Praise for *Rescued*

"Over the course of his priestly ministry, Fr. Riccardo has shown himself to be an outstanding communicator of 'the story' behind God's determination to get his world back through the radical gift of his Son, Jesus Christ. Fr. Riccardo explains with a simplicity that is at once eloquent and compelling how Jesus is the answer to the only finally important questions we all face. I am confident that those who read his presentation of the good news and thoughtfully respond to the questions he poses will be better equipped to join in the great work which the apostles once started—and now has been left to us in this generation: leading others to encounter Jesus, helping them grow as his disciples, and then launching them on the course of inviting others to make God's story for his world the story of their lives."

—Archbishop Allen Vigneron, Archdiocese of Detroit

"This is the book that I have been waiting for. If you read only one book this year, may *Rescued* be the one. Why are these words so needed in a world already saturated with information and opinion? Because we desperately need help making sense of the chaos we live in. Fr. John Riccardo offers exactly that. Read *Rescued* if you are longing for a clear perspective, if you need hope that things can change, and if you want practical wisdom to apply to the challenges you face. He not only explains why things are messed up but more importantly reveals the path to get back to a flourishing life. Fully engage with the truths in this book and you will be forever changed."

—Lisa Brenninkmeyer, founder of Walking with Purpose

"This book is a refreshing reminder of what God is doing for us in the person of his Son, Jesus. Not just for your head but even more for your heart, it will brighten your soul and restore your confidence in God's call upon your life."

—**Joshua Danis,** national director of Alpha Catholic Context and author of *Living the Fruit of the Spirit: How God's Grace Can Transform Your World*

RESCUED

THE
Unexpected
AND
Extraordinary
NEWS OF THE
Gospel

FR. JOHN RICCARDO

the WORD
among us®
press

ISBN: 978-1-59325-381-3
eISBN: 978-1-59325-382-0

Ecclesiastical approval for printing was granted by the
Most Reverend Allen H. Vigneron, Archbishop of Detroit, 29 October 2022.

Design by Suzanne Earl

Library of Congress Control Number: 2020913600

Contents

PART III: Rescued

PART IV: Response

Foreword

Once upon a time, we all believed our lives to be part of a larger story. It's a natural thing. When I tell the story of my life, I see a narrative arc, with clear high points and low points. I see cumulative development—emotional, intellectual, and physical growth. I assume that I came from somewhere specific and that I'm going somewhere—that I have a goal, though I glimpse it only dimly.

Civilizations also have stories. They *need* stories. Caesar Augustus knew this, so he hired the greatest poet of his time to write a backstory, a grand narrative. If Rome were to replace Greece as the world's dominant power, it needed an epic poem that could stand alongside *The Iliad* and *The Odyssey*. So Virgil produced *The Aeneid*.

Educated Greeks and Romans knew that these backstories were largely fictional. The myths made no corresponding demands on the people's everyday lives. They proposed virtues, such as patriotism and fortitude, but they enshrined no morals.

Biblical religion was essentially different from this. It ascribed its story not merely to human poets but to a God who is Creator, Redeemer, Lawmaker, Judge, King, and Guide. For Jews and Christians, the great story encompassed both the civilizational and the personal. It narrated the history of the people and the person. And they believed it to be history indeed—history that could be confirmed by the documents and monuments of the world. If they saw allegory in the biblical story, they saw it not merely in the words but in the events the words describe.

God writes the world the way human authors write words, and he composes creation and history to be a revelation of his life.

I came of age in a thriving evangelical Christian subculture, and I think its apostolic success came largely from its ability to tell the Big Story in a way that was at once universal and personal. We had four spiritual laws that outlined the narrative of creation, fall, and redemption. So it was intellectually captivating, and it was relatable. We pondered ways we could convey the story quickly—in the course of a plane trip or even an elevator ride. Even when I was a teenager, I saw adults change their minds and their lives because they suddenly came to an understanding of their past and future as part of God's plan.

Fr. John Riccardo understands this deep human need, and he recognizes that we live in a moment when every proposed alternative narrative is falling apart. Democracy and science can be good and great things, as far as they go, but they cannot save us. Their horizons are limited. They cannot supply us with a moral code. They are, moreover, dependent on metaphysical assumptions they cannot account for.

This book provides the simple account that's needed right now. The New Evangelization, heralded by popes since St. Paul VI, can go forward only by grace, but only insofar as we can tell our story in a compelling way. Fr. Riccardo does this. He distills the biblical narrative in a way that is simple but not simplistic. He implies the richness of Catholic tradition, which includes all the relevant sciences, and he sets up a conversation that can lead to a robust engagement of modern culture.

The key is at once very traditional and startlingly new with this book. It is the phrase Fr. Riccardo received one day in prayer: "ambush predator." When people stumble over the Christian story—now as in ancient times—it's usually because of the cross. "Nothing is so far above the reach of human reason as the mystery of the cross" (*Roman Catechism* I.4). How could this happen to almighty God? Where is the saving power in such abject weakness? Fr. Riccardo recovers the understanding of the first Christians, explaining how Jesus "will enter into Death and, from the inside, destroy its power. Jesus on the cross is not the poor, helpless victim, and he is not the hunted. Jesus on the cross is the aggressor and the hunter" (see page 114). In apparent weakness he lays his trap. He is himself the bait.

Our author marshals an impressive array of early Christian witnesses for this interpretive key: Irenaeus, Melito, Ephrem, and Maximus. And he lets them show us how to tell the story. Thus we learn not only from a master of modern preaching but also from the very voices who converted the world the first time around.

Though we sometimes wonder why God allows so much sickness, suffering, and evil, we take a look at the cross and we see the greatest evil ever perpetrated, the greatest suffering ever endured, and then the greatest gift God has ever given—the salvation of the human race.

We live at a moment when all other monuments are falling. We live in a time when so many other ancient documents, alas, are going unread or actually being banned for their civilizational associations. In some senses, this is a disaster to be mourned. At the same time, we must see it as an opportunity to be embraced. We have been created for this moment and called for this moment and so we will be empowered for this moment.

Ours is the story of Jesus Christ, and it is a story that encompasses all others and surpasses all others. It is a monument that will stand when all others have fallen. It is a narrative that will hold together when all others have unraveled.

It is the story told in the pages of this book, and I pray it will be retold by the readers of this book.

Dr. Scott Hahn, founder and president of the St. Paul Center for Biblical Theology and Fr. Michael Scanlan professor of Biblical Theology and the New Evangelization at Franciscan University of Steubenville

God Wants His World Back

> In the final analysis, specialized
> theological knowledge can take us only so far;
> we need to know the *story*.
> —Fleming Rutledge[1]

Why are you here? Not *Why are you sitting in your living room?* or on this airplane, in that school pick-up line, or in the office where you started working ten years ago. But why are you *here*, on the earth? Ever wonder where you're going or how you're going to get there?

We've just asked the three most important questions in life:

Why am I here?
Where am I going?
How do I get there?

Increasingly, many of us don't know the answers to and aren't even asking those questions. It's so easy to get caught up in life's daily grind: *What's for dinner? Are you going to the game? Should I quit this job? Maybe I should go to the doctor and get that spot checked out.* The daily questions, as important as they are, can also cause us to lose sight of the enormous questions: *Why am I here? Where am I going? How do I get there?*

Three Fundamental Convictions

I've been asking those questions. They have led me here, to this moment in my life, when I am driven by three fundamental convictions.

The first fundamental conviction is this: you and I are not alive *right now* by chance. God could have destined us to live in sixteenth-century France or in the Northwest Territory in the 1800s. Instead, in his mysterious providence, He chose you and me to be alive at this moment. Not in spite of but *because* of all that is happening in our local churches, the global Church, our country, and our world.

I am more and more enamored of a line attributed to St. Joan of Arc: "I am not afraid. God is with me. I was born for this!" I pray that wherever you are as you read these words, you will have the same conviction this heroic young woman had centuries ago: *you were born for this moment.* God is creating a masterpiece, and you play an irreplaceable role in this work of art. Whether you are a stay-at-home mom, a retiree, a high school teacher, a nurse, a cattle rancher, a truck driver, a lawyer, a teenager, or a grocery store clerk, *you matter.* Each of us is meant to be an instrument in his hands to help accomplish his desire. And his desire is nothing less than to get his children back and to get his world back.

The second fundamental conviction I hold is that the world is crying. To be sure, the world has been crying since that fateful day in Eden, but our current times are unique and unprecedented, at least in our country. There are many ways to speak to this conviction, but for me it started with a series of articles I read that reported that in 2018, for the first time in a hundred years in the US, life expectancy declined for a third consecutive year. This is astounding and hasn't happened since 1918. Think about that! Lives are shorter, and people are dying younger—not in some remote corner of the planet that lacks access to technology, wealth, and medicine, but here in the United States of America.

What was happening in 1918 that had caused life expectancy to decline three years in a row? Two horrors: World War I and the worst pandemic in the history of the world, the Spanish flu. But the current life expectancy decline in our country is due to something chilling and new. (At this writing, we don't yet know what the ultimate result of the coronavirus, or COVID-19, will be; however, the statistics I'm referencing were true even before the current pandemic crisis we've been experiencing.) Sociologists are calling the phenomenon "deaths of despair." There are three main causes of such deaths: suicide, cirrhosis of the liver, and opioid addiction.

Since 1999, suicide rates have risen 30 percent in the general population and 40 percent among rural Americans. In 2016, there were more than twice as many suicides as homicides in our country. The suicide rate among children ages ten to fourteen has nearly tripled in the last ten years. As I have, I'm sure you've been impacted deeply by this incredible pain, perhaps enduring the loss of a family member or a dear friend. I've lost both an uncle and a brother-in-law to this battle. I know firsthand the anguish and pain of those left behind after a suicide.

There's a second cause of our declining life expectancy. From 1999 to 2016, death by liver cirrhosis, due to alcohol addiction, increased 65 percent, with the biggest jump happening among young people ages twenty-five to thirty-four.

A third primary factor for a heartbreaking number of early deaths is the current opioid addiction. Despite being only 5 percent of the world's population, Americans consume 80 percent of the world's opioids. Deaths of despair are happening at a staggering, unprecedented rate.

At the root of this despair are those three questions I mentioned. In a world where God is repeatedly pushed further and further off the stage, the creature who is made in His image and likeness—you and me—has lost his sense of meaning.

Jesus instituted his Church to address precisely this kind of despair and to heal such wounds. He designed his Church to be the means by which the world's cry would be answered so that every person could come to know the incredible love of the Father, the regenerative power of the Holy Spirit, and their true identity as beloved sons and daughters of the King of the universe. The Church is intended to be the place where this is not merely heard but *experienced*.

The problem, which leads to my third fundamental conviction, is that the Church is crying too. Like the situation in the world, there are a number of ways to speak to this "cry" of the

Church. There are confusion and division amongst priests and bishops and confusion coming out of Rome. And most certainly, the second round of the sexual abuse crisis among the clergy in our country has made it abundantly clear that we are wounded and weeping. A recent Gallup poll revealed that 37 percent of Catholics are considering leaving the Church due to the sexual abuse scandal.[2] With roughly seventy million Catholics in the US, that translates to twenty-six million people who are hurting, scandalized, and disillusioned. *The Church is crying.*

For many who serve in parish or diocesan life, whether as priests or lay men and women, there is also the experience that parish life is not quite what it could and should be. Too many days are spent playing "whack-a-mole." With fires raging daily, we grow accustomed to having our heads on a swivel, bouncing from emergency to emergency. One person has suggested that working in the Church reminds them of a football game: there are twenty-two men desperately in need of rest racing around the field, and they're being watched by thousands of people in the stands who are desperately in need of exercise.

I recently finished a twelve-year stint as pastor of an extraordinary parish in the Archdiocese of Detroit. I'm grateful for the people I was blessed to walk with during this time, even though serving a parish with nearly 3,600 families can be stressful. My archbishop graciously allowed me to create a new ministry, ACTS XXIX, but before that began, I was able to take a month off to recharge. Around the third week, I realized I was suffering from what I can only call some type of post-traumatic stress. I'd gotten so used to racing from one trauma to another, day after day (almost hour after hour!) that I didn't realize how desperately I needed a break. Countless priest friends, not to mention lay men and women who serve in parishes, are suffering through the same experience right now.

In these times, then, when both the world and the Church are crying, what is the way forward? How do we move beyond such immense discouragement?

Recapturing the Big Picture

Would it surprise you to read that I'm not discouraged but am actually encouraged, even excited? That might sound crazy, but I like challenges, and I love a good fight. Clearly, God didn't want you and me to live in a time that is dull and monotonous. He wanted us to live *now*. He has equipped us with everything we need to be instruments in His hands in order to share the gospel. These are not dark days but great days to be alive. God is not nervous or anxious; He's chosen you and me for this moment.

Of course, I don't presume that I have *the* answer for our next steps, but I do think that the book you're holding is the most urgent answer. Or perhaps I should say that it's what God has put on my heart to share with everyone I can because I believe it to be the most important thing *right now* in the fight for God to get His world back. Why? Because with every fire raging in the country, the world, and the Church, there is an urgent need to pull out of the weeds and recapture the big picture, to acquire again (or perhaps for the first time) a biblical way of seeing reality. As author and minister Fleming Rutledge said, "We need to know the *story*."[3] So let's begin by viewing reality as God has created it, through the lens of Scripture.

CHAPTER 1

The Whole Story

In order to reacquire that biblical worldview and grasp its principles, we must see the world through a specific set of lenses crafted by God and designed to give us 20/20 vision. To gain that vision, we must ask the fundamental questions: *Who is God? Why did He make everything? Why is it all so messed up? What, if anything, has He done about it?*

These questions are especially necessary for many of us who have grown up Catholic. We have to ask ourselves, "Do I regularly hear the gospel at Mass?" I don't mean Matthew, Mark, Luke, or John; we hear those every week. I mean *the gospel*—the incredible, life-changing proclamation of what God has done for us in Jesus.

In Romans 1:16, St. Paul said, "For I am not ashamed of the gospel; it is the power of God for salvation to everyone who has faith, to the Jew first and also to the Greek" (NRSVCE).

The gospel is *power for salvation*. And what does salvation mean? Health, healing, freedom, wholeness. Like Humpty Dumpty, we fall off the wall every day. In our fragile humanity, we crack and split and are broken. God picks up the pieces and tenderly puts us back together again in a way that nothing and no one else can. So we start fresh and whole again every day, and one day we can become everything God created us to be. This is salvation.

The proclamation of the gospel, then, is power. The word Paul uses for "power" in Romans 1:16 is the Greek word *dunamis*, from which we get the word "dynamite." In other words, the gospel—what we know as "the good news"—is not just news, but it's *extraordinary* news. It's explosive, life-changing news. At least it's *supposed to* be, but I don't think that's how most people experience it because most people don't hear it preached in its fullness. *They don't know the story.*

Sometimes, as I sit in church, I look around at people's faces, and I wonder what they're thinking. One day, the Lord offered me an intriguing image. I felt as if I had just put on those special lenses He crafts to clear our vision. As I looked around at the sea of faces, I thought, *It's as if these people just woke up in the middle of chapter seventeen of a novel. They have no idea they're in a novel, let alone what the other chapters are about, who the author is, or what the plot is. They're lost; they don't know what's going on.*

It isn't their fault, and I'm not blaming my brother priests or deacons, but it's happening every week in Masses everywhere. *We don't know what's going on during Mass.* Countless people are left thinking, *Oh, here we go again. That Old Testament reading that I don't understand. And this Gospel parable about the unjust steward that Jesus praises? I never understand this one either. I hope the priest doesn't ramble too long this week. Maybe he'll be funny today—that always helps. I hope he gives me something concrete to take with me. I'm really tired this morning.*

That's not what the word of God is supposed to accomplish. It's supposed to be *changing my life.*

God's Plan for the World and Our Mission in It

In *Evangelii Gaudium*, Pope Francis's letter on evangelization, he says that the gospel is "the message capable of responding to the desire for the infinite which abides in every human heart."[4]

This is why the message of the gospel is perpetually relevant: because we all have the same desires; we want infinite love. We want to have a sense of identity and to be accepted. We want to know that our lives have meaning. We want to know that we matter. In short, we want *happiness.* God has a monopoly on happiness, and He made us to share in his own happiness forever.

Each of us is meant to be a herald of the gospel. But that can scare us. We don't feel confident that we can share, preach, or tell our stories, much less tell God's story to others. But what Paul is saying is that *the gospel itself is power.* The power doesn't come from us, the messengers, but rather, the message itself changes lives, regardless of how well or how badly we communicate it.

St. Joan of Arc knew that. She's often quoted as saying, "I am not afraid. God is with me. I was born for this!"

So what happens when we stop being afraid and the word of God *does* change our lives? Pope St. John Paul II once wrote that the result of hearing the "ardent proclamation" of the message of the gospel is that "a person is one day over-whelmed" and comes to the decision to surrender himself in faith to Jesus.[5] Think about that for a moment. Have you been personally overwhelmed by the message of the gospel? Have most churchgoers you know been overwhelmed by the gospel? Have you or those around you at Mass surrendered your lives to Jesus in response to the unexpected and extraordinary things He has done for you? Sadly, even as a priest, I can become used to talking about the good news as if it were mundane.

Someone once wrote that nothing is worse than getting used to the magnificent. I don't think, however, that most people have gotten used to the magnificent. Rather, I think they've never heard the magnificent in a concerted, dramatic, and pow-erful way. God's magnificent message, when genuinely heard and experienced, *overwhelms*. And after that, there's no turn-ing back, nor would we want to.

Why Are They There?

How then are we supposed to hear and really grasp this news that is meant to shake up our lives? Let's imagine a couple of scenes.

It's June 6, 1944, in Normandy, France. Military forces from the United States, England, and Canada have converged in Europe and are landing on five separate beaches. Why are they there?

Is it because they've heard that the beaches in France are awesome? Or that the coffee on the Champs-Elysées, on the main street of Paris, is to die for? Maybe it's because they're chomping at the bit to see the *Mona Lisa* at the Louvre after hearing so much about her. No, of course not. The Allies are storming the beaches in France for a single reason: to fight. A tyrannical dictator has invaded, oppressing and killing people for his own megalomaniacal purposes. They are there to fight this monster.

Now imagine another scene: a manger in a cave in Bethlehem. A young Jewish woman named Mary has just given birth. She is holding her baby; her husband, Joseph, is by her side. They gaze upon the child who has just landed on this earth. Now ask a similar question: "Why is *He* there?"

Do we have as quick and obvious an answer to that question? Perhaps not, but we should. Because once we understand why God became a man in Jesus and what He came to do, we feel compelled to surrender to Him in faith.

Let's return for a moment to the first scene we conjured up. Imagine you live in France in 1944. Your country is occupied, and you have family members who have been kidnapped and sent to a concentration camp. You live every agonizing day under the shadow of the Nazi regime, dwelling in darkness and the shadow of death. You wonder if you will be saved— if you and your people *can* be saved from the tyrant who has invaded your land.

Then, on June 7, 1944, you wake up, get the newspaper, and sit down with your spouse at the kitchen table. You open the paper and see the massive headline: The Allies Landed at Normandy. Your spouse asks, "Anything happen yesterday?" You reply, "Nah, not really. The Allies landed on our western shores to rescue us, but that's about it. Looks like it's going to rain today."

Is that how you'd read the headline? Not a chance!

"*The Allies landed!*" you'd exclaim. "They're here to *fight* for us! To *rescue us*! The horror can finally end!" You would weep with joy, relief, and a hope for the future that you'd stopped dreaming was possible. Because this isn't just mundane, every-day news; this is *the* news—extraordinary, life-changing news. In France on June 7, 1944, everyone knew that something unprecedented had happened. It was *the* event that changed everything for them from that day forward.

As great as that news was, the gospel—the proclamation of what God, who knows you by your name, has done for you and me personally—is *infinitely better.* And it's longing to be unleashed through you and me, by our words and by our actions.

Just as the Allies landing on D-Day presupposes Hitler and the Nazis, God becoming flesh in the person of Jesus presup-poses an enemy. And just as the Allies didn't come to France to see the sights or drink great coffee, God didn't land as a tourist. He became a man to fight.

People don't usually ask to meet with me in order to say, "Hey, life is great, Father, and I just wanted to share that." Instead, most people who request to sit down with a priest do so because they're in crisis. Given this, I've learned to ask those people a simple question before we continue our discussion: "Can I take five minutes to explain how I see the world? Because if I don't do that, the rest of what I say won't make sense." Then I try to help the other person see that I view the world through a par-ticular set of lenses that give me a biblical vision of reality.

Here's an example. A while back, I met with a young woman. She was stunningly beautiful, wealthy, and professionally successful, but interiorly, she was a mess. Before we continued our talk, I asked if I could share with her the lenses through which I view the world. She agreed, and five minutes later, she was overcome with emotion. Weeping, she looked at me and said, "That's not the God I knew growing up. I've never heard that before."

We are surrounded every day by people like that young woman who, through no fault of their own, don't know who God is. They've simply never heard the life-changing news. Maybe you're one of those people, or maybe you love someone like that. Whoever you are, know that God *want*s to reveal Himself—*to* us and then *through* us. How? By way of the unexpected and extraordinary news of the gospel.

Unpacking the Gospel: Easier Than You Think

The gospel is referred to in several ways. First, of course, there's simply the word we've been using, which you've probably heard translated as "good news." And the gospel *is* the good news. But sometimes words become so commonplace as to grow meaningless to us. *Nice, fine, adequate. Yeah, good stuff. Is it going to rain today?*

No. The gospel is not simply "good" news that we read or hear once, only to return to the weather forecast. It's explosive news, the best of news, the news that should be splashed on the front page of every newspaper. It's the headline revealing that our eternal ally has landed. We can certainly keep calling it the time-honored "good news," but don't let those words lose their meaning.

Another word you might have heard to refer to the gospel is *kerygma*. *Kerygma* is simply a Greek word that means "proclamation," as in "the proclamation of the gospel." The kerygma has traditionally meant telling God's story using these four components:

- the goodness of creation,
- Sin and its consequences,
- God's response to our sin, and
- our response to what God has done for us.

That sounds a bit academic and doesn't inspire the kind of overwhelming feeling that Pope St. John Paul II described. So I rephrase the kerygma into four questions:

- Why is there something rather than nothing?
- Why is everything so obviously messed up?
- What, if anything, has God done about it?
- If God has done something, how should I respond?

As we hear the gospel and strive to share it, we need an even easier, more concise way to remember what the kerygma—the proclamation of the gospel—is. So I've shortened it into four words:

- Created
- Captured
- Rescued
- Response

If you know those four words, you know the gospel! So let's dive in.[6]

Next, we'll take a closer look at what's behind the first of the four words, "Created."

Summary of Introduction and Chapter 1

- The three most important questions are: *Why am I here? Where am I going? How do I get there?*
- You are not alive right now by chance. God has destined you for this moment.
- Clear vision calls for a particular lens: a biblical worldview. We need to know the story.
- The gospel is not merely good news; it's the most extraordinary news we can imagine.
- The kerygma (proclamation of the gospel) can be summarized as *Why is there something rather than nothing? Why is everything so messed up? What, if anything, has God done about it? How should I respond?*
- Even more concisely: Created, Captured, Rescued, and Response.

Discussion Questions

1. Through what lenses do I view reality? Why?
2. Have I ever really thought about the question "Why am I here?"

3. Have I been personally overwhelmed by the message of the gospel and surrendered my life to Jesus? If so, how did that happen? If not, why not, and what might it take for that to happen?

PART I

Created

As we dive into the gospel together, our goal is not merely to learn something, but to *experience* something—in short, to let God overwhelm us. In these pages, I hope less to teach you than to act as a companion who wants to help you encounter God (or help you to help someone else encounter God). As you read the chapters that follow, ask God for that encounter. Ask Him for specific graces to accompany you as you ponder what it means to be created, captured, and rescued, and to respond.

As you read Part I, "Created," ask for the graces of wonder and trust.

CHAPTER 2

In the Beginning

Lift up your eyes on high and see:
who created these?
He who brings out their host by number,
calling them all by name.
—Isaiah 40:26

The traditional presentation of the kerygma, or "gospel message," has always invited us to first consider the goodness of creation. "But," you say, "that phrase hardly overwhelms me, as Pope St. John Paul II said should happen!" As I mentioned in the last chapter, perhaps we can rephrase it to ask, "Why is there something rather than nothing?" Does that still feel a little too academic? Let's whittle it down to the bare bones: Created. And let's ask the Holy Spirit for the grace to be overwhelmed and filled with awe, wonder, and trust as we break this word open.

What does it mean to be created? When human beings consider where they came from and why, what conclusions can we, or should we, reach?

It's less complicated than you think. Let's start "in the beginning" with the book that God gave us—the Bible—and take a look at the absolute uniqueness of the creation accounts in Genesis. I'm convinced that if we get the first three chapters of Genesis right, we understand the whole story of salvation correctly. If we get those wrong, we can miss everything. We'll focus on these things:

- how to approach Genesis,
- the uniqueness of the creation stories in Genesis,
- God's grandeur, and
- the wonder and trust that come from knowing God.

Before we dive into Scripture, I want to mention a practical point. Did you know you can write in your Bible? I learned this from my mother, who always left her Bible out on the kitchen table for all to see. Even as a child, I was struck by the fact that she didn't treat the Bible as an heirloom but, rather, as something she wanted to dig into deeply. After my mom passed away, one of my sisters received that Bible. She regularly texts me pictures of Mom's margin notes—snapshots, if you will, of something the Lord revealed to Mom in prayer or a verse she wanted to remember.

As a result of my mother's example, I write notes all over my Bible—and you can too! If you're going to be a student of Scripture, feel free to act like a student. Underline words, leave question marks next to confusing passages, and circle whatever jumps out at you. When there's something you don't understand, make a margin note, or slap a sticky note on it so that you can return to it. Scripture can be confusing, so don't be afraid to mark up your Bible and ask questions. You're not going to hurt God's feelings by writing in His book. He wants you in those pages, so get your highlighters ready.

Going to the Library

I have a friend named Joe who is perhaps the country's leading expert on Mark Twain. If you told Joe you wanted to learn more about Twain's books and what made them successful, one thing he might point out would be the importance of foreshadowing. You know how sometimes you read a great book and only when you get to the end of the story do you realize how many clues were front-loaded? "Oh, my gosh!" you say. "I've got to go back and reread chapter 2!" Suddenly, you see that a throwaway line was actually a pivotal plot clue. That's foreshadowing.

Just as authors use foreshadowing in literature, God uses it in Scripture. Scripture is full of the kind of foreshadowing that we call "typology." ("Types" are people, places, and events in the Old Testament that foreshadow those to come in the New Testament, especially the coming of Jesus.) The first three chapters in the Bible are jam-packed with it: clues, hints, and even major spoilers of what will play out in profound ways later on, especially in the life of Jesus. God is the greatest author, so it's not surprising that the drama He created, lived, and revealed to us in Scripture would include expert foreshadowing.

The challenging thing about reading Scripture is that it's not a book. Scripture is a library. It's not one genre; it's a boatload of genres. Just as a modern library has contemporary fiction, classics, biographies, romance, and "how to" books, Scripture has myriad sections and shelves. Those shelves hold historical narrative, poetry, apocalyptic literature, and even a love song right smack in the middle. Precisely because the Bible holds a variety of literary styles within its pages, we have to be mindful when we're reading it. There's no Dewey decimal system to point the way, so we need to ask, for any given book, "What genre is this?"

A document called *Dei Verbum* (which is Latin for "Word of God") is helpful. You might find this document in the front of your Catholic Bible, or you can easily find it online. (Just search for "Vatican II Dei Verbum.")

Dei Verbum is short, easy to read, and downright reassuring. Paragraphs 11 and 12 are particularly helpful in guiding us about how to read the Bible:

> For holy mother Church . . . holds that the books of both the Old and New Testaments in their entirety, with all their parts, are sacred and canonical because written under the inspiration of the Holy Spirit, they have God as their author and have been handed on as such to the Church herself.[7]

This is just confirming that God is the author of Scripture. Next, pay close attention to the points that immediately follow:

> In composing the sacred books, God chose men and while employed by Him they made use of their powers and abilities, so that with Him acting in them and through them, they, as

true authors, consigned to writing everything and only those things which He wanted.[8] . . . However, since God speaks in Sacred Scripture through men in human fashion, the interpreter of Sacred Scripture, in order to see clearly what God wanted to communicate to us, should carefully investigate what meaning the sacred writers really intended, and what God wanted to manifest by means of their words.[9]

The Church is telling us that Scripture needs to be "carefully investigated." Casual reading won't cut it, and a superficial reading won't always make sense. And finally, *Dei Verbum* declares,

To search out the intention of the sacred writers, attention should be given, among other things, to "literary forms." For truth is set forth and expressed differently in texts which are variously historical, prophetic, poetic, or of other forms of discourse. The interpreter must investigate what meaning the sacred writer intended to express and actually expressed in particular circumstances by using contemporary literary forms in accordance with the situation of his own time and culture. For the correct understanding of what the sacred author wanted to assert, due attention must be paid to the customary and characteristic styles of feeling, speaking and narrating which prevailed at the time of the sacred writer, and to the patterns men normally employed at that period in their everyday dealings with one another.[10]

In other words, "Pay attention to what you're reading because it was authored in a particular time and place using a variety of literary forms." Remember, when the Scriptures were being written, it wasn't as if someone had a pen and scroll and scribbled down dictation, stopping God occasionally to say, "Okay, God, hang on and slow down. I'm out of parchment."

Scripture is *not* the result of dictation. So, when we read Scripture today, we have a twofold challenge. First, we're twenty-first century people. Second, we are Americans. We don't see the world the way the Middle East sees the world. When we try to read ancient texts with a twenty-first century American mindset, it doesn't work. We have to wrestle with these texts in order to understand them clearly.

Scripture study is vital, and it takes effort. You don't have to have a PhD in Scripture to be able to read the Bible, but sometimes it feels like you do! You're skimming along, and suddenly things get muddy. You want to throw up your hands and shout, "I don't know what this book is talking about. Help!" Everyone who reads the Bible, and perhaps especially the first few chapters of Genesis, feels this way. You're not alone, so I'm going to simplify the process for you.

We need to ask ourselves two simple questions: "What style, or genre, am I reading? Is this, for example, a science book?" The other question is "Is this how the contemporaries of the Jewish people saw the world?" We are going to look at those two questions in regard to Genesis and—here's some foreshadowing—it's *not* a science book, and it's *nothing* like what the contemporaries of the Jews saw the world to be.

Name That Genre

Before you dive into the Bible, remember: your first question is always "What style am I reading?"

I'll share an answer that a wise mentor and Scripture scholar gave me. He said that the best way to approach Genesis 1–11 is as inspired poetry. This is a style of writing that speaks truth, but it communicates that truth to us in poetic language.

Maybe the thought of "poetic language" makes your head explode, especially if you're an engineer or a mathematician. Most of us think of "truth" as cold, hard scientific facts. But that's a diminished understanding of truth. If the only truth is that which is made up of scientifically repeatable facts, and if the world is understandable only through mathematical formulas, how do we prove intangibles like love? Is love unprovable? Of course not. We know that love is real. We just can't verify it by the scientific method.

The initial chapters of Genesis, then, are poetry, and they communicate truth to us in a rich and diverse way. That's immediately helpful because the first three chapters of Genesis, especially the stories of creation and the fall, are not easy to believe on the level of "cold, hard scientific facts." Which is why many people, both in and out of the Church, think or fear that to believe the Bible means we have to check our intelligence at the door. "How am I supposed to believe," they ask, "stories about a world made in seven literal days, a woman made from a man's rib, a talking snake, and that eating some fruit led to the downfall of the entire human race? Are you Christians crazy or just stupid?"

We're not crazy, we're not stupid, and we can all relax because we're not taking those stories literally either. When we read the Bible, we see that *Scripture itself* tells us not to read these chapters literally. Let's repeat that: as Catholics, we do not read everything in the Bible literally. A literal interpretation applies to many stories and events in the Bible, but we have to be mindful of the genre employed before we determine whether or not a text is meant to be taken literally. The genre of Genesis is poetry. Remember what *Dei Verbum* told us:

> To search out the intention of the sacred writers, attention should be given, among other things, to "literary forms." For truth is set forth and expressed differently in texts which are variously historical, prophetic, poetic, or of other forms of discourse.[11]

In the poetic literary form used in Genesis, the form itself practically screams, "Don't read this literally."

Let's look at two cases that prove this point.

Does God Make Gaffes?

Do you know how many versions of the creation story are in the Book of Genesis? Two. One is in the first chapter; the other is in the second. There are *two separate stories of creation, back to back, and they are not identical!* It's not as if the divinely inspired writers and editors of Scripture just missed that fact or made a publishing gaffe. It's not that they threw in a variety of versions just to cover all the bases and hoped we wouldn't notice. There's a reason for the variation. It's a subtle way of saying, "Don't read this literally." God, the ultimate author, is considerately saying to His readers, "That first chapter didn't work for you? Let's add this one. This one will help you understand."

Here's another section that tells us not to interpret the story of creation literally. We read:

> And God said, "Let there be lights in the firmament of the heavens to separate the day from the night; and let them be for signs and for seasons and for days and years, and let them be lights in the firmament of the heavens to give light upon the earth." And it was so. (Genesis 1:14-15)

> And God made the two great lights, the greater light to rule the day, and the lesser light to rule the night; he made the stars also. (1:16)

> And God set them in the firmament of the heavens to give light upon the earth, to rule over the day and over the night, and to separate the light from the darkness. And God saw that it was good. And there was evening and there was morning, a fourth day. (1:17-19)

As I mentioned earlier, people sometimes challenge the Bible's authority by asking, "Are you guys so stupid that you think that the earth was actually created in seven twenty-four hour days?" Here's one way I often respond: "I'm stupid about plenty of things, but that's not one of them. No, we Catholics don't believe the world was created in seven twenty-four hour days. Actually, the Bible *itself* tells us that they were *not* twenty-four hour days."

"Huh? Where does the Bible say *that?*" Genesis says that the sun and moon were created on "the fourth day." How, precisely, would we get "a day" without a sun? We wouldn't, and we didn't because it's impossible. Days, as we know them, did not exist until the sun and moon were created and set in motion. Clearly these are not literal days. The story of what happened on each "day" is another way in which Scripture urges us, "Don't get lost in the minutiae. Don't focus on what the authors are *not* trying to communicate to you. Focus on the truths that *are* being transmitted to you." God is not revealing *how* everything happened. He's revealing *why* it happened.

Misunderstanding Scripture's genres gives rise to fruitless debates about things like creation versus evolution, but there's no need for such debate. The real debate—the crucial question—is about creation versus chaos. Either everything that exists is here for a reason, or everything randomly appeared. Which do you believe? Creation or chaos? And why?

The Whole Human Person

So the early chapters of Genesis were written in poetic language. My friend Joe, the Mark Twain expert, and I were both English majors. When we hear the word "poetry," we're on board, ready to analyze, discuss, and go the whole nerdy nine yards. But maybe when you hear the word "poetry," you think, "Sheesh, why am I reading this? I *hate* poetry." Stay with me. When you grasp what I mean by poetry, it will change everything.

Poetry is actually just a manner of speaking to the whole human person in a way that a scientific formula cannot. As important as science is—and the Church has tremendous respect for science because it helps us understand truth—it has a limit. Science can't answer the most important question of the universe: *why*? Only the author of the universe can tell us *why* there is something rather than nothing. And He does that.

Let's come at it from one other angle and compare two ways of speaking. I want you to imagine someone you love. Now imagine expressing your love to that person using only objective, mathematical, or scientific terms. It might sound like this: "I am experiencing something in relation to you that is characterized by feelings of warmth, closeness, and affection. As a human being, I am programmed to live in community, and it's in my DNA to form attachments to other people. I sense such attachment to you. Various hormones are involved as well, and I may occasionally act in a way that seems contrary to reason, perhaps even responding with giddiness. I believe the term for this is love."

Think that will win the heart of the man or woman you love? I doubt it.

More likely, you'd walk hand in hand with your beloved, bursting with gratitude and wonder for this relationship and all the riches it has brought into your life and find yourself saying, "I love you. You mean everything to me. You've changed my life, and I can't imagine a world without you."

That's the difference between scientific explanations and poetry. As we get deeper and deeper into Scripture, we'll find that it is more like a love letter from God to the whole human person than a newspaper article detailing events. And that's the beauty—and the genius—of the word of God.

CHAPTER 3

The Uniqueness of the Genesis Creation Story

Now that we know to view the early chapters of Genesis through the lens of inspired poetry, we need to address the second question: *Is this how the contemporaries of the Jewish people saw the world?* Let's compare the first chapters of Genesis with the creation stories, also referred to as creation myths, of the ancient Near East.

Myth, in this context, doesn't refer to a fictitious account of reality. More accurately, it's an attempt to describe reality in its entirety. When we hear the word "myth," we might imagine a cyclops or a centaur and scoff, "None of that stuff is true." But that's not what we mean when we use the word "myth" here. As a wise friend of mine says, at its core "myth" means "a meaningful story or an overall narrative that makes sense of existence."

When I was at the University of Michigan, I took a class in mythology. I loved the class, but I didn't love hearing the professor assert that all ancient cultures have creation stories that are essentially the same. I assure you: that assertion is absolute rubbish. No other myth has anything like the creation stories that are found in the first two chapters of Genesis.

There are many strikingly different stories of creation in the ancient Near Eastern myths, but in general, their attempt to address the question "Why is there something rather than nothing?" looks roughly like this:

- There are many gods.
- These gods aren't even in control—they are subject to something greater, often called some version of "the fates."
- The gods are violent, lustful, greedy, and capricious.
- The gods create men to be slaves so that they can rest.
- Women have no dignity and were created solely for childbearing and man's sexual pleasure.

These creation myths present gods who act, well, just like us. They're greedy, lustful, spiteful, angry, and constantly at war with one another. They are awful and obvious projections of human beings.

At a certain point in these creation stories, the gods created man to be a slave. Since the gods were always on the lookout for leisure, they wanted someone to take on their labor, leaving them free to loaf, act on their lust, or just hang out. Women, regarded as utterly mentally and physically inferior, existed only for reproduction and male pleasure, with no evidence of their dignity as human beings.

The dominating worldview as well as the conclusion of such myths is that we human beings have no inherent dignity. How could we? When the creator is eclipsed, the creature loses all intrinsic dignity. If we were incidentally created by the gods to be playthings, those gods will pay attention to us only when they feel the urge to be entertained, as a child might view ants on a sidewalk through a magnifying glass.

Imagine that world. You came from nowhere, you're going nowhere, and you're daily scuttling about doing the work you've been programmed to do. There's no ultimate purpose to marriage, family, or sexuality. There's not even purpose in the work you're doing—you're just like that ant, fulfilling your duties in the colony and only occasionally being noticed by the gods who find your endless labor amusing.

What reigns in a world like that? Despair. Meaningless-ness. Hopelessness.

When the answers to the questions *Why am I here?* and *Where am I going?* are *no reason* and *nowhere*, creatures stop asking the next meaningful question: *How do I get there?* That's not a relevant question when you're on a train to nowhere in a world that lacks all meaning.

So what do you do? How do you live? You minimize pain and maximize pleasure. If you're going to live by the rules of the reality you've been handed—that *nothing really matters*—you exploit other people, and they exploit you as everyone pursues the most pleasurable existence possible. It's every man for himself. Why waste your time with kindness, integrity, and being good? You're not going anywhere, and there are no consequences beyond this finite world, so the goal becomes: *enjoy yourself!*

That's the ancient world I've been describing, and I would argue that it's the worldview that dominates our culture today. In other words, if society decides God doesn't exist, human life has no meaning.

Image and Likeness

In contrast to that bleakness, consider the worldview presented in Genesis:

- There is only one God.
- He's *good*. He is complete. He needs nothing outside himself.
- God created everything out of nothing—freely, effortlessly, and generously.
- Everything He created was made out of love.
- Everything that God created is *good* (and He tells us that repeatedly).
- The highlight of everything God created is the human person, made in His image and likeness.
- Man and woman are created absolutely equal in dignity; only *together* do they *fully* reflect God's image.
- The end, the purpose, and the reason every human person was created is to be divinized.

Regarding God's goodness, note one other important point from Genesis, which we'll return to later. This is from the sixth day of creation:

And God said, "Let the earth bring forth living creatures according to their kinds: cattle and every creeping thing and beasts of the earth according to their kinds." And it was so. And God made the beasts of the earth according to their kinds and the cattle according to their kinds, and *everything that creeps upon the ground* according to its kind. And God saw that it was good. (Genesis 1:24-25, emphasis mine)

Don't forget this bit of foreshadowing! What "creeps upon the ground"? Snakes. In the third chapter of Genesis, a snake will emerge, and that serpent will become the antagonist of this entire story. He's the reason everything went wrong. But remember this glorious truth: there is only one God, and He is good. The enemy is not a "rival" to God; he is only a creature.[12]

Next, in Genesis 1:26-27, we read something extraordinary: "Let us make man in our image, after our likeness; and let them have dominion."

What a stark contrast to the ancient Near Eastern worldview, in which the gods created man to be a slave! In the biblical worldview, humans are created *in God's own image and likeness*. What in the world does that mean? Let's unpack it.

First, it means that, of all creatures, man is somehow able to—*meant* to—represent God on earth. This doesn't refer to a bodily representation—that we look like God or that He looks like us. It means that man is somehow supposed to *make God present on earth*. That is the vocation of the human being.

Second, God commissioned man to exercise dominion over the earth. This is sometimes misinterpreted to mean domination over or exploitation of the earth, but that's wrong. Dominion means we are stewards of all of creation, entrusted with the responsibility of caring for the earth. A steward is in charge of something that belongs to another. Since everything belongs to God and we're His stewards, it logically follows that an ecological focus on caring for the earth is a vital part of the Church's teachings.

Third, to be made in the image and likeness of God, who is the inventor of reason, means that we too have the capacity for reason. This is a vital point. Jesus, through His Church, wants us to grow not only in faith but in *reason*. Our culture often divides people into two categories. On the one hand are people who are intelligent, logical, and reasonable, and on the other hand are silly, uneducated, and unreasonable people of faith. But to have faith is not to be naive or illogical. After all, the Church was at the forefront of the establishment of universities and higher education! The Church has always believed that the more we employ intellect and reason, the more we can learn about God, who is revealed in countless ways in His creation.

Faith is not blind, but it is a way of knowing. It is different from scientific reasoning but not in contradiction to reason. This is immensely important. We live in a time of very little critical thinking and a whole lot of emotional yelling and name-calling. The reasonable way, however, to approach crucial issues is to learn, examine various sides of arguments, take time for discernment, and then allow the truth, not feelings, to lead us forward.

Fourth, being made in God's image and likeness means that we have the capacity for freedom. Human beings are free in a way that no other creature on earth is. Animals don't have freedom; they operate from instinct. A dog can't be disobedient.

You can take him to obedience school, but the lessons don't endow the dog with free will. They simply retrain an instinct in him. We have instincts too, but we don't have to act on them. We have both the intellect and the free will to make informed choices. We can feel extraordinarily annoyed by something or someone, but we have the power to put on a polite face and interact in civilized ways. We might get enraged and, in the midst of that anger, think, *I'd like to kill that guy!* But we don't have to act on our feelings or on our most base instincts. Human beings have the freedom to determine what's right and then to act on that.

Humans and angels are the only creatures who have that capacity to choose obedience or disobedience to God.

Freedom From and Freedom For

In our current culture, "freedom" is a loaded and often misunderstood word. It's important for us to reclaim and understand that word rightly. We think of freedom as the capacity to do whatever we want whenever we want. But that's not real freedom—that's lawlessness. For example, you can't simply choose to drive on the wrong side of the road on the way home. If you're an alcoholic, you can't simply choose to drink to excess; your addiction leads you to an enslavement in which you no longer make free choices. That's not freedom; that's a set of shackles.

Genuine freedom is not only freedom *from,* but it's freedom *for.* Being free *from* restraints means being free *for* clear-eyed choices. An alcoholic must be free *from* inebriation in order to make the choice *for* sobriety. If he's still bound by the shackles of alcohol, he isn't making real choices; he's just sitting in his prison.

I once had a friend who was a crack addict. He suffered like few people I've ever known. In the short time I knew him, he sold his furniture, his car, and even his body just to get his next hit. The day he sold all their furniture, he and his wife came to see me. She was livid, and she expressed her anger and frustration. He looked at her and, crying his eyes out, said, "Do you think I like this? That I want this? I hate this! I'm stuck, and I don't know how to change!" He desperately needed and wanted to be free *from*.

What, then, is the purpose of human freedom? God created us free primarily so that we could love. Without love, we cannot be truly happy. I can't say to someone, "You *must* love me." That wouldn't be love. Only someone who is free can genuinely love. And that's why God made us—the angels and human beings—free.

Male and Female He Created Them

Genesis 1:27 reads, "So God created man in his own image, in the image of God he created him; male and female he created them."

If I were standing in front of you delivering a talk right now, this is one of those moments when I'd say, "Listen up! This is *huge*!"

I could write a whole book on this particular truth revealed in Genesis, but for now, let's focus on this: men and women not only image God as individuals but also together as man and woman. Man and woman, though different and distinct, are equal in dignity and worth. And like everything else God created, that's *good*.

The ultimate foundation for this is the Trinity (another topic worthy of its own book) because God is three Persons—Father, Son, Holy Spirit—and They are *equal and yet distinct Persons*. In the same way, we are all made in God's image and likeness; therefore, we are equal ("male and female he created them"— Genesis 1:27) but distinct. Neither one is better than the other. We are simply different.[13]

But there's a problem with that. Since the fall of humanity in the garden, our world has often been governed and normed by, not just men, to the exclusion of women, but by *bad* men, deformed men who don't understand what it means to be human. Seeing the "success" of these men, women have sometimes imitated "men behaving badly," and as a result, things are more than a bit messed up. The point of life is not to amass money, power, and pleasure, all the while exploiting everyone in our path. The purpose of life is to be loved and to love. Nothing else will ultimately satisfy us. We desperately need healed men and women to bring their unique perspectives into our messed-up situation.

Unique, In Need, and Made for Eternity

Genesis 1:28 goes on to say, "God blessed them, and God said to them, 'Be fruitful and multiply.'"

Two things about this passage point to the particular nature of human beings in the world that God has created. Have you noticed that there is a difference in how God addresses the animals and how He speaks to humans? In Genesis 1:22, after creating the creatures of the sea and air, we read, "And God blessed them, saying, 'Be fruitful and multiply.'" But in Genesis 1:28, after the creation of man and woman, we read, "And God blessed them, and God said to them, 'Be fruitful and multiply.'" This subtle difference in language is another indication of the absolute uniqueness of the human person. And note that sexuality is blessed, thereby revealing that marriage and sexuality are part of the divine plan, contrary to the ancient Near Eastern creation stories, in which neither marriage nor sexuality had any ultimate purpose.

In Genesis 1:29, "God said, 'Behold, I have given you every plant yielding seed.'"

This reminds us of one more simple but important point: the fact that human beings need food means we are, by definition, dependent beings. We are not self-sufficient. We *need* to receive. It's a defining characteristic of humanity: we are *one giant need*. But God knows this and takes pleasure in providing for us and cares for His creatures by giving us all that we need. He's a good Father.

Finally, note too that nothing dies in paradise. God created, He provided, and—in the beginning—Death was not part of the game.

So this first creation account ends in chapter 2, verse 2, with these words: "On the seventh day God finished his work which he had done, and he rested on the seventh day." This highlights the importance of the Sabbath and, contrary to popular images of God as a rigid, stern taskmaster, tells us that God also loves to play. We are not created only for worship and work, but for rest, refreshment, leisure, and play. Again, He's a good Father, providing for us all that we need. And this good Father is also a mighty, all-powerful God who loves us beyond anything we can comprehend or imagine.

CHAPTER 4

God's Grandeur and Reckless Love

So far, we've covered how to approach Scripture, the uniqueness of human beings made in the image and likeness of God, and our capacity for reason and free will. We've looked at the amazing complementarity of men and women, the nature of humanity as beings in need, and God's provision as a good and generous Father. All of this can be summed up in a few simple words: God made us to be loved and to love. That's where true happiness comes from.

To be loved and to love. Importantly, it's in that order: being loved by God came first. So we can stop scheming to win God's love, as I did for so many years. Many of us go through life worrying, "I hope I'm good enough to please God and win His love." Know this: *nobody* is good enough. But God loves us anyway. That's why we call his love a gift.

But what kind of being loves so richly, so generously, and with such grandeur? Who is this God who created everything? To answer that, let's return to Genesis 1. Hopefully, as we look at one simple verse, we'll be filled with wonder, awe, and trust in the One who made us to be loved and to love.

Genesis 1:16 is a passage that's easy to skim over. Until last year, even I didn't pay much attention to it! But increasingly, I find it to be one of the most extraordinary and humorous passages for contemplating God's grandeur. The passage begins, "And God made the two great lights, the greater light to rule the day, and the lesser light to rule the night." That refers to the sun and the moon. Then, almost as an afterthought, it continues, "He made the stars also."

I picture the writer of this passage putting quill to parchment and writing, *He made the sun, He made the moon.* Then I imagine him looking up, pondering, as if he's forgotten something. Suddenly it comes to him: *Oh yeah! I almost forgot. He made the stars.*

Excuse me? *He made the stars also.* Do you have any idea how many stars there are?

Let's talk about stars. If we really think about a being who is capable of making stars, we realize that God is *incomprehensible.* This passage is one of the most incredible and helpful ways to break open that concept.

The universe is ninety-plus billion light years across (in miles, that's forty-six billion multiplied by almost six trillion). Our sun is one of roughly *one hundred billion* stars in our galaxy. And there are roughly a hundred billion galaxies in the universe. I don't know about you, but I'm not sure what to do with those numbers. I get lost in them. A hundred billion stars in a hundred billion galaxies—how big *is* this? And the author says, "Oh yeah, He made these too. I forgot to mention these few quadrillion things."

When an English major like me hears numbers like that, my brain hurts. How can we better grasp what is being revealed? I once heard a high-energy particle astrophysicist, who was giving a talk on the grandeur of God, explain the magnitude of these numbers. He said, "Imagine a sandcastle where every grain of sand is a star in the universe. How big would the sandcastle have to be to replicate the size of the universe? It would be thirty-five miles long, thirty-five miles wide, and thirty-five miles high."

That's mind-boggling. I'm a visual person and wanted to better visualize this, so one day I went out and drove that distance. Picture it: I'm driving along with my head out the window, trying to "see" thirty-five miles up in the air, which is roughly equivalent to the tallest mountain on the planet. So there I am, driving thirty-five miles from my church, and then thirty-five miles over, then back, and the whole time, I was looking up, just trying to grasp this image of a massive sandcastle in which every grain of sand is a star. Staggering.

Here's another image that might help. Our sun is a relatively small star, and yet our sun could hold roughly 960,000 Earths. One of the largest stars in the universe, Canis Major, (which is Latin for "The Big Dog"), could hold seven quadrillion Earths. *Seven quadrillion.*

And what's a quadrillion? If our heads haven't exploded yet, let's try to grasp that.

If you started right now to count to one million, it would take you eleven and a half days. If you counted to a billion, it would take you thirty-one years. If you tried to count to a trillion, you wouldn't make it because it would take you thirty-one thousand years. Counting a quadrillion seconds? Thirty-one million years!

Have you gotten a handle on a quadrillion? You can fit *seven quadrillion* Earths inside Canis Major, and that's just one of hundreds of billions of stars in a universe that's ninety-five billion light-years across and ever expanding.

Oh, yeah. He made the stars. I almost forgot to mention that.

What are the ramifications for us of this enormous, mindboggling, and brain-rattling universe?

There is one very important ramification: in this universe that is massive beyond our understanding, the creature God loves more than any other creature is *you*. It's not "us" or "humanity in general." God doesn't see numbers and crowds. He sees *individual human beings*. He knows our *names*.

That's why every single human person is so important to the Church.

As I'm sure many of you do, I remember vividly where I was on 9/11: an airport in Chicago, about to board a plane to Minneapolis. On a TV, I saw what looked like a plane flying into the World Trade Center. Suddenly utter chaos broke out. People were screaming, and police were everywhere. We were rushed out of the airport, onto buses, and I was taken to a hotel. As I waited for a friend to pick me up, many of us huddled around a TV in the hotel lobby, watching the horrific events unfold. A network anchor was in the middle of an update when someone handed him a note. He read it and, with great sadness, looked into the camera and said, "I just learned that one of those planes was flying from Boston to Los Angeles. I'll bet there were some important people on that plane."

Some important people? I'll never forget those words, and I was amazed at his gall. He was probably imagining celebrities, athletes. What about the teachers, the stay-at-home moms or dads, the receptionists, the police officers, or the plumbers on that flight? There are *no* unimportant people. We are alive simply because God willed us into being. We are *all* important people to God. He knows everything about you and me. Not because He's spying on us through a keyhole but because He—the God who breathed this incomprehensible universe into being with no effort whatsoever—is also a Father who cares about you and about me beyond anything we can imagine.

To Be Loved and to Love

In the introduction, we talked about the three most important questions in life: *Why am I here? Where am I going? How do I get there?*

The answer to all of those is one word: love.

Why am I here? Because the Creator of this massive, incomprehensible universe, the God who simply breathed, spoke, and willed entire galaxies into existence, chose to create me. I don't just "happen" to be here, and neither do you. We're here because God created us, out of his love.

Where am I going? You, who were made in the image and likeness of God and are the highlight and pinnacle of everything He made, are meant to be divinized. That's your destiny and the destiny of every human person. You're meant to share forever in God's own abundant life, joy, and happiness. That's where you're going.

How do I get there? We get there by love—God's love for us, fully revealed in the life, death, and resurrection of Jesus, and by our loving response to God and love for each other.

The Bible as Healing Balm

A friend of mine used to say that the Bible is healing. The story of our creation, unique in all of time and space, transmits a healing balm to us. Tonight, if you can, go outside and take a look at the stars. Try to count them. Remind yourself that there are *hundreds and hundreds of billions* of stars. Know that the God who willed all of them into being has *your* life, as well as the lives of all those you love, in His hands.

Does that alter your conception and image of Him?

Perhaps when you pray, you have an image of God in your mind, as I often do. We nervously wonder if God can "maybe" or "possibly" do something to answer our anxious prayers about our lives, our country, our Church.

"Maybe"?

Know that whatever limited images our minds can create, they are wrong. God, who is never nervous, anxious, or worried but is powerful and majestic beyond all understanding, holds your life firmly in the palm of His hand.

Picture the struggles in your life—illness, anxiety, relationships, financial trouble, and all the things that keep you up at three in the morning—and know that you can relax.

Really. "Cast all your anxieties on him," Scripture tells us, "for he cares about you" (1 Peter 5:7).

God created and runs this immense universe, and nothing is more important to Him than you and me. He can take care of our lives. Trust Him to do so. The Creator of the universe knows and loves you, not only when you're "behaving" and doing all the things He tells you to do, but *all the time*. He wants to say to you, "You are my child. I *love* you. Your life is in My hands. Don't be afraid."

Before you started this chapter, I encouraged you to pray for the graces of wonder and trust. Do you feel them? Do you sense God's immensity and power? Do you feel His love and really believe that you matter to Him?

You do. He thinks you're worth the trouble.

And that's what it means to be created.

Summary of Part I: Created

- Scripture is a library; know what genre you're reading.
- There is one God, He freely chose to create, and everything He made is good.
- We, the human person, are the highlight of His creation, made in His image and likeness.
- We have reason and free will, which render us capable of genuine love.
- We were made for relationship (with Him and with each other); our destiny is to be divinized and partake of God's nature.
- God is more powerful than anything we can comprehend.
- Real happiness means to be loved and to love.

- Understanding God's nature (both His immense power and intimate love for me) leads to wonder and trust.

Discussion Questions

1. What am I anxious or fearful about right now in my life? Is my life filled with confidence and trust or am I riddled with anxiety and fear?
2. What effect does contemplating the grandeur and magnificence of God and His personal love have on me and on my fears?
3. What is my image of God now?

PART II

Captured

As you read Part II, "Captured," ask for the grace of despair. (That may sound odd or hard; rest assured, I'll talk more about that later.)

CHAPTER 5

What the Hell Happened?

When we consider the human condition, we picture two players on the stage: God and me. And if something goes wrong, whom do we blame? We like to point the finger at God. In our lives, however, there are actually three persons on the stage: God, you/me, and another. Who is the other? In this chapter, we're going to move from the wonder and awe that flows from "Created" to "the bad news." We'll ask the Holy Spirit to shine a brilliant, cleansing light and expose the key player, that third actor on the stage in our human drama. He is our enemy, the one who ultimately holds the blame for everything that's gone wrong.

Before we dive into the second part of the kerygma, "Captured," I want to share a word of warning and a word of hope.

First, the warning: this was *not* a fun section to write, and it will not be a fun section to read. But please hang in here with me. I am convinced that the reason many people don't think of the gospel as unexpected and extraordinary news is that they don't know or understand the "bad news." We rarely hear about it at Mass, and the secular media doesn't talk about it either. But the bad news isn't just bad; it's horrific. If we don't grasp what would have happened to us had Jesus not rescued us from our captivity, we miss what is extraordinary about the gospel.

Second, and most importantly, is the hope. As you read this section, remember that there is only one God and that He is good and without rival. We can and need to explore the horror of our captivity precisely because God Himself has revealed these truths to us. Read this section in trust, not fear, because God is in control of exposing the enemy. The Lord is the One shining an intense light on him, revealing his identity, how he works, and what our situation has been since the fall. I liken the Lord's light to an aircraft landing light. You know how blazingly bright those lights are? They cut through fog and darkness and show the pilot exactly what he needs to see. In this chapter, God is shining that blazing, brilliant light on the enemy, exposing him for what he is, and breaking through the darkness in order to give us clear vision.

To further encourage you in hopefulness, remember this helpful image: Scripture is "game film."

In Part I, I talked about the Bible as a library. Scripture is like a video library too. If you've ever played football or know someone who has, you know that coaches record games and use that film ("game film") to train their players. A successful coach shows his team what its opponents are doing. He prepares them for possible plays and points out where the enemy is weak. That's the key to excelling in sports: get to know your opponents extremely well! Learn their strategies and tactics, and be on guard for what's coming next. When you know where your enemy is weak, you can expose that weakness and immobilize him. You can *win*.

That's what Scripture does. Scripture is game film. Through it, God shows us what to expect from the enemy, what his weaknesses are, and how we can overcome his attempts to conquer us.

Scripture doesn't simply tell us what happened once, long ago, in a biblical era far, far away. Scripture tells us *what always happens*. Because what the devil did to Adam and Eve, he's still trying to do to us today. That's a sobering reality. For example, in my life, Satan has been running the same play for more than fifty years, and sometimes it feels like he keeps getting nine yards, running that same play over and over. Fortunately, I'm finally getting better at the game, but first I had to recognize what was happening. I had to learn from the game film.

The more we understand about the enemy, the more we see what plays he's running in our lives. God exposes those strategies and equips us for the game in which our souls are at stake because He wants us to win.

Here's the game film we'll be breaking down: we'll look at the consequences of sin and the fall, which are different than what you might have previously understood them to be. And we'll take a close look at the enemy and expose everything about him. We'll look at

- his identity,
- his reason for rebelling,

- his names,
- his root strategy,
- his tactics, and
- his goal for our lives.

The grace to pray for as you read this chapter is despair. As we delve into the painful truth of what it means to be captured, I invite you to pray for this grace. I know this sounds odd, but stay with me. Of course, despair is not a virtue, and I'm not encouraging you to plummet into despair. Rather, we want to ask God to help us understand how hopeless our case would be if He had not done something in His Son, Jesus, to rescue us from our captivity. Ask God for the clarity and grace to understand just how bad this bad news really is. So come, Holy Spirit, and enlighten us as only You can. Help us to see why everything is so obviously messed up, and help us understand that our race has been captured.

But as you read, always remember trust and hope: God *has* done something. We *do* have hope, precisely and specifically because of *what* He has done.

Let's get started.

CHAPTER 6

Enemy Territory

The first part of the kerygma, or "gospel," was "the goodness of creation." I summarized that as *Why is there something rather than nothing?* and even more simply as "Created."

Part two of the kerygma, "Sin and its consequences," can also translate into *Why is everything so messed up?* And my one word summary about Sin and its consequences for humanity is this: "Captured."

Knowing that a good and loving God created us out of sheer love and wants us to be happy, do you ever wonder how it all went wrong? We know that there is only one God. We aren't living in that Marvel comic universe I mentioned, rooting for the good god to beat the bad god. We know there's only one God and that He's good, but if He's so good and so powerful, why is everything so obviously and thoroughly messed up? Why do children die? Why is there human trafficking? Why is there abortion, abuse, and cancer?

To put it more bluntly—and I mean every word of this— *what the Hell happened*?

I came across a quote not long ago from a very prominent priest. Unfortunately, here's what he said: "Symbols are part of reality, and the devil exists as a symbolic reality, not as a personal reality." With all due respect to my brother priest, who I'm sure is a holy man, he is wrong. And my authority for saying that is Jesus Himself. Jesus was not culturally bound by the times in which He lived. He spoke often about the reality of the enemy and the ways we must face him in the world. The devil is no mere symbol. He is real. God wants us to know this and to understand the nature and character of this creature who is fighting against us, and He has the perfect means to expose the devil and his tactics: Scripture. Remember, Scripture is game film!

Identity: Who Is He?

Since there is one God who is good and loving and effortlessly made everything out of love, how do we explain where evil comes from? Evil comes from one of the creatures that God made: an angel whose name was Lucifer, which means "light bearer." Lucifer was created to be good. As the *Catechism of the Catholic Church* reminds us,

> The Church teaches that Satan was at first a good angel, made by God: "The devil and the other demons were indeed created naturally good by God, but they became evil by their own doing."[14]

God wants us to understand that Satan is not God's equal or a rival on the same plane; he is merely a creature. God created both angels and human beings to have free will, but God did not create evil. However, now that evil exists, God uses Scripture to teach us about how that creature, "at first a good angel," went wrong, how he factored into the fall of the human race, and how we can thwart him.

The story begins in Genesis:

> Now the serpent was more subtle than any other wild creature that the Lord God had made. He said to the woman, "Did God say, 'You shall not eat of any tree of the garden'?" (3:1)

This passage emphasizes that the enemy is just a creature, as we are. Remember, God wants to keep the enemy in his place. This is some game film, showing us our opponent's nature.

Have you ever read C. S. Lewis' book *The Screwtape Letters*? If not, I highly recommend this phenomenal and humbling book. It's about a "senior" demon giving advice to a "junior" demon. The senior tempter explains there are two main strategies: to get humans to think the devil isn't real or to get them to believe he's more powerful than he really is. The devil is an angelic creature, which means he *is* a more powerful creature than you or me, which is why Pope St. John Paul II exhorted us to "have nothing to do with the dragon." In other words, don't flirt with Satan or dabble in the occult because an angelic creature is beyond what we can fully grasp. On the other hand, he is still merely a creature, and his power is limited. He is not another god.

Let's look at what Scripture says about his identity. The story begins in Genesis, chapter 3, the rebellion, or fall, of Adam and Eve:

Now the serpent was more subtle than any other wild creature that the LORD God had made. He said to the woman, "Did God say, 'You shall not eat of any tree of the garden'?" (3:1)

Again, the point is just to say that the serpent, the devil, is a creature. God is keeping him in his place.

There are many texts we could look at to help us understand the enemy's identity, but we'll just look briefly at a few in the New Testament and start with how Jesus identifies him. Shortly before he entered into his Passion, Jesus said, "Now is the judgment of this world, now shall the ruler of this world be cast out" (John 12:31).

In identifying the enemy as "the ruler of this world," Jesus was not naively blaming evil on some supernatural power that doesn't exist. He was not an ignoramus who didn't know better, nor was He spouting outmoded, superstitious ways of thinking about Satan. Jesus dealt with concrete and eternal realities, and He called Satan "the ruler of this world." He spoke to us—and continues to speak through Scripture and the Church—about that third player on the stage, and we do well to listen to him.

The rest of the New Testament is chock-full of references to the enemy. St. Paul called him "the prince of the power of the air" (Ephesians 2:2); Peter exhorts us to be constantly on guard since "the devil prowls around like a roaring lion, seeking some one to devour" (1 Peter 5:8). And John puts it simply: "The whole world is in the power of the evil one" (1 John 5:19). Some scholars say the biblical worldview of the early Church—expressed in Paul, Peter, John, Jude, and others—simply takes as a given the reality of the devil and his attempt to ruin God's creation.

Most people don't live with that same biblical worldview. Many naively imagine that we were born into some sort of neutral territory, when in fact you and I were born in a war zone and into a battle. And the first step in surviving and then winning a war is knowing that you're at war.

So this "prince" is identified in Genesis as a serpent. (Remember, the early chapters of Genesis are inspired poetry and therefore often make use of imagery.) There are a lot of reasons for the serpent imagery, not the least of which is that snakes look slow, blend in, and can seem harmless if you don't know what they're capable of. In fact, they are remarkably fast, strike out of nowhere, and can be lethal. It's such a powerful metaphor for Sin: it looks harmless but it kills.

In the last chapter, we looked briefly at this bit of foreshadowing:

And God said, "Let the earth bring forth living creatures according to their kinds: cattle and creeping things and beasts of the earth according to their kinds." And it was so. And God made the beasts of the earth according to their kinds and the cattle according to their kinds, and everything that creeps upon the ground according to its kind. And God saw that it was good. (Genesis 1:24-25)

The author of Genesis specifically mentions "everything that creeps upon the ground" in the context of goodness to remind us that God made everything, nothing is outside of His control, and all of it was made good.

Let's fast-forward our game film to the final book of the Bible:

The great dragon was thrown down, that ancient serpent, who is called the Devil and Satan, the deceiver of the whole world. (Revelation 12:9)

In the final book of the Scriptures, God reveals to us the creature who was introduced in the first book of the Scriptures. He helps us understand that this creature once dwelt in heaven. He connects the dots for us, and the finished picture shows that the serpent was a good angel, created by God and given an intellect, will, and reason. This creature, like all of the angels, was endowed with the capacity to love. He was created to love God, to worship Him, and to be in community with the other angels. That's who he is and was meant to be, but he rebelled.

Scripture, from beginning to end, is equipping us to face this enemy while also reminding us that he is just a creature, not another god. Unfortunately, he is a powerful creature and who will wreak havoc on your life if you are not connected to Jesus.

What Are His Names?

In Scripture, names mean something. They reveal a person's character or mission.

The enemy, as we saw, was originally named Lucifer, or "light bearer." Now, after his rebellion, he has two primary names. These names also reveal his character and they reveal what he does. His first name is Satan (the accuser) and his other name is the devil (the divider). There are many biblical references to these names. Revelation 12:9 calls him both. Ephesians 6:11 tells us to "put on the whole armor of God, so that you may be able to stand against the wiles of the devil." And 1 Peter 5:8 warns us to "be sober, be watchful. Your adversary the devil prowls around like a roaring lion, seeking some one to devour." But remember that when a lion roars, he's just trying to scare his prey. Don't let him scare you.

What's His Reason for Rebelling?

Why did this creature, created out of love and goodness, rebel? This isn't often understood well. We usually hear that Satan's motive for rebellion was pride. It's true that pride is his *sin*, but according to Scripture, his *motive* for rebelling is not pride, but envy:

> Through the devil's envy death entered the world,
> and those who belong to his party experience it. (Wisdom 2:24)

So why did he choose to leave the angelic courts behind and do what he's doing now? Envy is the motive behind the rebellion. This is immensely important! When this sinks in, everything changes.

What's envy?

It's not the same thing as jealousy. At times, jealousy can actually be a good thing. Jealousy can help or motivate us. For example, if I see someone living a healthy life or a holy life, I can rightly say I'm jealous of that, I want that, and I should aspire to holiness and healthiness too. Jealousy can move us to a better life, so there's not necessarily anything objectively wrong with it.

Envy, on the other hand, is one of the capital sins, a deadly sin that leads to other sins. It is never good or helpful. Envy is the sadness we feel over the good fortune of another. Envy makes us so sad, in fact, that we wish the other person didn't have the good fortune they're experiencing. It's pathetic, really, when another person's joy causes us such sadness. Envy doesn't act as a catalyst to virtue, as jealousy can. Rather, it's a self-centered, self-serving sadness that fuels the desire to take goodness and joy away from the other.

I used to think I was never envious of anyone. Then I realized, humiliatingly, that I'm envious *all the time*, even over things like sports! I actually rejoice when teams I can't stand lose the game, and I lose sleep when "my guys" don't win. I'd like to say I used to be that way—I'm still that way! Maybe you can relate?

That's envy. And who is the enemy envious of? You and me. Not of God. This creature, whom Jesus calls "the ruler of this world" (John 12:31), is envious of *us*, which means he hates us.

Why does he hate us? A friend of mine, in trying to help us understand how this mighty, majestic, and perfect creature could possibly decide to rebel against God because of what God promised human beings, wrote this to me:

> [The devil] perceived that in fulfilling the role God had planned for him, according to heaven's logic of love, he would be called upon to serve [human beings] of far less power and excellence

than himself. He envied the good that he saw coming to them, and he resented their destined place. The sight of these happy creatures filled the devil and his fallen angels with anger and envy, and so they took thought as to how they might mar the work of God and destroy the destiny of this newly created race. They set about to enslave those whom they had been meant to serve and to degrade those who had been assigned such an exalted place into the lowly slime beneath their feet.

In other words, in the demonic logic, to see us lifted above the angelic ranks was so abhorrent to Lucifer and the others who rebelled that they wouldn't stand for it. They will never want to serve us. It would never be an insult or a degradation, but he perceives it that way. So he instead reverses that and wants to enslave and degrade the beings he was intended to serve. That's Hell's strategy: to enslave and degrade.

The moment this clicked for me, everything changed about how I understood the devil and Sin. *Destroy. Enslave. Degrade.* Calling him "the enemy" suddenly makes so much more sense.

So envy is what fueled the enemy to rebel, and he invited other angels to join him. Revelation says,

His tail swept down a third of the stars of heaven, and cast them to the earth. And the dragon stood before the woman who was about to bear a child, that he might devour her child when she brought it forth. (12:4)

Woe to you, O earth and sea, for the devil has come down to you in great wrath, because he knows that his time is short. (12:12)

In its style of inspired poetry, Scripture is telling us that a third of the angels rebelled and went to war, not against God, but against us. Satan and other rebellious angels are our enemies, and they comprise a malign force beyond what we can comprehend.

The motive is envy. The fight? It's with *us*.

CHAPTER 7

The Enemy's Root Strategy and Tactics

We've identified the enemy, what he is called, and why he rebelled. Now let's take a look at his strategy and tactics. Satan has one root strategy and one play that he repeatedly runs in our lives. He tries to convince us that God is not a good Father but, rather, is our adversary. Satan tells us, again and again, that we can't trust God, that He doesn't care for us, and that we'd be happier without Him.

This was the lie he told to our first parents, Adam and Eve:

He said to the woman, "Did God say, 'You shall not eat of any tree of the garden'?" And the woman said to the serpent, "We may eat of the fruit of the trees of the garden; but God said, 'You shall not eat of the fruit of the tree which is in the midst of the garden, neither shall you touch it, lest you die.'" (Genesis 3:1-3)

The enemy makes this seem like a harmless conversation. The serpent casually states, "So God said you couldn't eat of any of the trees of the garden . . . " He's trying to engage Eve in a conversation, but he has an ulterior motive. Why does he approach it this way?

Imagine two people in a friendship, and then imagine that I have a malevolent intention to split them up. Call them Greg and Rachel. They're talking in the break room at work one day, and then I walk in and Rachel leaves. And even though I wasn't any part of their conversation, I casually say, "Hey, Greg, did Rachel mention anything odd to you? I'm not sure she's trustworthy. Just sayin'." If Greg truly trusts Rachel, he'd say, "That's ridiculous. I know Rachel, and she's completely trustworthy." But my ulterior motive is to catch Greg off guard and plant suspicion. I want him to say, "What makes you say that? Tell me more." It's like a fishing expedition. And that's what the enemy did. He was hoping the woman would bite. He wanted Eve's ears to perk up and get into the conversation. Tragically, she did.

She tells the serpent that God had told them they could eat from every tree except one tree, and she even adds something God didn't actually say. She tells the serpent that God said they should not even touch the tree.

> But the serpent said to the woman, "You will not die. For God knows that when you eat of it your eyes will be opened, and you will be like God, knowing good and evil." (Genesis 3:4-5)

That's the heart of Satan's strategy: to convince us that God is not a good Father, that we can't trust Him, and that we can be happy without Him.

Pope St. John Paul II, in a letter on the Holy Spirit, wrote,

> God the Creator is placed in a state of suspicion, indeed of accusation, in the mind of the creature. . . . [The enemy] seeks to "falsify" Good itself. . . . For in spite of all the witness of creation . . . , the spirit of darkness is capable of showing God . . . as an enemy of man. . . . Man is challenged to become the adversary of God![15]

Pope St. John Paul II reminds us that in Eden, our first parents, Adam and Eve, knew perfection. There was no sickness, no pain, and no Death. No loss of a friend or family or objectification. Just perfection. And yet this creature, Satan, was able to cast God in suspicion and to get our first parents to doubt that He's good.

When God told Adam and Eve not to eat from the tree of the knowledge of good and evil, He was acting as a good Father. What happens when you eat something? You take it, you break it down, you appropriate it, and you make it yours. You "own" it. In the inspired, poetic style of Genesis, God is telling us that to "eat" something is to have mastery over it. And if God's creatures eat from the tree of the knowledge of good and evil, it means they are appropriating for themselves the right to determine what is good and what is evil. We can't do that. Only God can do that.

Essentially, in protecting Adam and Eve from the tree of the knowledge of good and evil, God was saying, "You have to trust Me in this relationship. If you no longer trust Me, you cut yourself off from life—because *I am* life—and the result is that you'll die." God didn't *want* them to die. It wasn't that He got incredibly angry and railed, "Now I'm going to smite you because of what you've done!" Rather, the necessary consequence of "making yourself God" is that you choose to cut yourself off from Him. It's like a mother saying to her child, "Don't put your hand on that hot stove. I know it's red, pretty, and tempting, but if you touch it, you'll get burned." If the child chooses to touch the stove anyway, the resulting burn is not because the mother got angry and administered a burn herself; it's that touching a hot stove has a consequence.

Our first parents experienced the consequence of their actions because Satan got them to wonder about God's trustworthiness. They questioned God: "I think He's holding out on us. He's repressing us. We might be happier apart from Him." God was cast in suspicion, and Satan accused Him of being a bad Father and our adversary.

Satan is capable of convincing us that God is an enemy. Don't underestimate this because if he could do it with Adam and Eve, he can manipulate us too. With all our unanswered prayers and the hardships we've endured, natural disasters, pandemic illness, and the loss of loved ones, Satan's voice rings in our ears: "You think He's a *good* God? You must be kidding. Where's this 'good' God? He's nowhere. He's silent. He's impotent. *He's not there.* Be done with Him, and you'll finally be happy."

Why does he do that? Because he hates and wants to degrade and enslave us in any way he can. So he casts God in suspicion and accuses God of lacking love. It's a lie. But all too often, we fall for the lie, seeking happiness apart from God.

Satan's root lie—that God is not our loving Father and that we can be happy without Him—took root in Adam and Eve. The third chapter of Genesis lays out Satan's game plan succinctly and clearly. Back it up, rewind, watch that game film again, and learn from it.

Remember, Scripture doesn't simply tell us what happened once, long ago, in a biblical era far, far away. Scripture tells us what always happens. Satan is still telling the same old lies to you and me.

What Are His Tactics?

How does the enemy employ his root strategy and spread his root lie? He uses many tactics, but let's highlight these:

- he accuses,
- he lies,
- he divides,
- he flatters,
- he tempts, and
- he discourages.

Let me break all those open for you by sharing something from my life. When I was a child, I was sexually abused for years. I came from a phenomenal family; my parents, who were married for sixty-six years, were my heroes. But no one knew about the abuse: not my parents nor my sisters. I can't begin to describe the wound that abuse left in my life. I am fifty-four years old as I write this, and the grown man in me understands certain things, but the little boy who was abused can't understand how those things happened. More than a few of you reading this know this experience. We all have trauma—trauma is not unique to anybody, but some of you know *this* particular experience. One of the reasons I talk openly about it is so that you will talk about it too. Go see the Lord, talk to Him about this, ask Him to help you, and seek professional help as well.

Let me just walk you through how the enemy used this abuse in my life. Mainly, he accused. He accused God, he accused me, and he accused those who are closest to me.

First, he accused God: "Why didn't He stop this? When you prayed for Him to help you, why didn't He help? He's not *good*. Or maybe He's weak. Or He just doesn't care. Maybe He's *not even there*."

Then he accused me. The enemy's play is always to accuse the victim: "This was *your* fault. You did this. *You* brought this on." We all know a child doesn't "bring this on" and is *never* responsible for abuse, but when the enemy whispers those accusations in a child's ear, the child doesn't know the truth. A wounded child believes that twisted message.

Finally, in my mind, he accused my parents: "They don't love you. They never did a thing to stop this, and your siblings? They don't care either."

I sat down with my sisters several years ago to finally share what had happened to me. They never knew until I told them. I said, "I know you love me. The fifty-four-year-old man knows you love him, but the six-year-old boy in me thinks you had no concern at all for him, and now I have to fight that feeling every time I see you because the enemy's voice is so strong."

When he's done accusing, the enemy lies. The lies go something like this: "You don't matter. You're worthless and disposable. No one cares about you. If they knew the truth about you, they would run from you. You will never be loved."

Then, the enemy divides. When you feel those lies so powerfully, it hinders your ability to enter into relationships because you're so accustomed to the lie that "no one really cares." You believe that all anyone wants is to use you, and he repeats that lie over and over again. So you can't enter into a new friendship because you're afraid this friendship too will end when he or she learns the "truth" about you, which is that you are discardable and disposable. This cycle keeps you alone, which keeps you enslaved. Because without love, life is meaningless.

Next, the enemy flatters. Flattery does not honor another human being. Flattery is simply saying something to someone in order to get something out of that person. A mentor of mine once said that most people, despite their facades, don't think they have much good in them (and that's often because of things that happened to them when they were young). Our task as human beings is to find the good in others, hold it up to them, like a mirror, and affirm, "You have good in you and I see it, and I just want to tell you that." That's honoring another human being. Flattery, on the other hand, is using someone to get something. The enemy flatters by saying things like "You know, you had all this bad stuff happen to you, and you've endured a tremendous amount of pain; so you are entitled to_____." Then we fill in the blank of what we think we're entitled to.

The enemy tempts. That one is pretty obvious. We all understand temptation. And finally, he discourages. That's the foundation of all of this. The devil's game is to get us into a hole. He doesn't really care how; he just wants to get us into a hole where he can taunt, mock, and humiliate us.

He employs these tactics with all of us incessantly. And by the way, because he's an angel, which means he's a pure intellect, he doesn't sleep! But this is when we remind ourselves that he is just a *creature*. He's not another god. God doesn't want us to sink into fear! Remember, it is God who is exposing this knowledge to us. He is shining that brilliant landing light on the devil's tactics so that we can go on the attack.

Now that we're aware of Satan's root strategy and tactics, let's examine his end goal.

CHAPTER 8

Satan's Goal for Your Life? Destruction

Satan's goal is simple. He wants to steal, kill, and destroy. And it's personal. He has all the game film on my life, your life, and thousands of years of human history. He knows what works, which is why, ultimately, he isn't terribly creative or original.

The Consequences of Sin: Slavery

What are the consequences of the fall? Oftentimes when people teach the kerygma, they say that the consequence of Sin is that you and I were separated from God. When I was seventeen years old, if you'd said, "John, the consequences of Sin are that you're separated from God," I would've responded with a yawn and then a resounding, "Big deal! I'm my own man. Who cares if I'm separated from God?" But the key is that we're not merely *separated* from God. We are either in the hands of God or in the hands of this other being. There's no middle ground. This is the biblical vision of reality. We can't just hang out in some nebulous playground, planning to choose later.

The most powerful way I've ever experienced this was when I was doing the Spiritual Exercises of St. Ignatius. St. Ignatius, who founded the Jesuits, taught people the methodology that God taught him and that led him to his encounter with God. It's usually done in a thirty-day retreat in which you spend hours every day praying and meditating on different scenes of Jesus' life. It's very rich, but sometimes extremely difficult, as it was the day I did a meditation on Hell.

St. Ignatius taught that we can use our imagination to pray and "get into the scene" as best we can. To be clear, the motive for this particular meditation on Hell is not to torment us, but to cultivate gratitude for all that God has done. So I asked the Holy Spirit to take me to the moment of my judgment.

In my imagination, the Lord brings me to an auditorium, where I see Jesus. Time has ended; He's come back in majesty and glory, and everyone can see that He really is God. Everybody is in line waiting to be judged, and I'm at the end of the line. Individually, people are approaching Jesus. One by one, Jesus looks at them, His face erupts into a smile, and He says, "Oh, well done, My good and faithful servant. Wait, just wait, until you see what My Father has prepared for you." Each of them hears the same thing. "Well done, My good and faithful servant." And this goes on, over and over. I'm the last guy in line, and I'm walking up to Jesus, but now . . . Jesus has His head down. And when I reach Him, the smile has evaporated. He looks at me with this tremendous sadness. And He says to me, "Depart from me, you cursed, into the eternal fire prepared for the devil and his angels" (Matthew 25:41).

Then I watch Him walk away from me, toward a door. I hear the door open, and Jesus walks out. The door closes behind Him. I hear the latch click. He is gone, and I am standing there all alone on the stage. I start to panic. There's no chance to say I'm sorry, no opportunity to run to Confession, no time to repent. Time is up. And I realize I'm absolutely and utterly alone forever.

Then as I'm standing there, I hear someone in the back of the auditorium laugh. And I realize I'm *not* alone. This thing walks closer and closer to me and then finally stands in front of me. And this creature says to me, "You *fool*," as he laughs. "God offered you abundant life, and you fell for my lie. Oh, just wait until you see what *I* have prepared for you."

When we die—not "if" but "when"—we're going to hear one of those two things. We'll either hear, "Well done, good and faithful servant" or "Depart from Me."

Life is best lived backwards. Let me explain. I've found it helpful to apply a lesson from the game of golf to life. Here's how most people play golf: they stand at the tee and swing as hard as they can. Then they head off down the fairway trying to find the ball. When they find it, they hit again (and again and again!) Finally, they get the ball on the green and into the hole, and then they head off to do it all over again. Great golfers don't play that way. Great golfers stand at the tee and ask themselves, "Where do I need to be on the green to make the putt?" and then they say, "Where do I need to be in the fairway to hit the shot onto the green to make the putt?" Only then do they consider their tee shot. That's how we best live life—backwards. We start living well by asking the question "When I die, what do I want to hear?"

That's a no-brainer, right? I want to hear "Well done, good and faithful servant"! If that's what I want to hear, how do I live my life so as to hear that when I die and stand in front of God?

The reality of the consequences of the Sin of our first parents is that unknowingly they sold us into slavery to powers we can't compete against. What are these powers? Death and Sin. (I deliberately capitalize the words here in order to emphasize their towering claim on us.) Death isn't just something that happens to us, and Sin isn't just the things we do. In the biblical vision of reality, Death and Sin are powers. Scripture talks about them as if they are governments, or authorities. They have dominions and they rule.[16]

It's easy to prove that Death has dominion over us. I buried my mom, my dad, and my brother in the span of two-and-a-half years. I remember standing at my mom's bedside, watching her breathe her last. My father had left us plenty of money, but that didn't matter. I couldn't stop Death from happening. We had great health care. That didn't matter either. It couldn't stop Death. If you've stood at the bedside of a loved one, watching him breathe his last, you know there is nothing that makes you feel more impotent than knowing you can't stop his death from happening. Why? Because Death is a power. It's a kingdom.

And Death is here because of Sin. Here's how Fleming Rutledge put it:

RESCUED

Have you ever buried someone? If you haven't, you will. You will come to know the cold clasp of death. . . . It will seem to you like the tomb of hope.[17]

Death is constantly hovering over us and those we love. All the people I love are either going to say goodbye to me, or I'm going to say goodbye to them, and that hurts. As playwright Samuel Beckett said, "They give birth astride of a grave, the light gleams an instant, then it's night once more."[18] And as William Stringfellow said, "Death is so great, so aggressive, so pervasive and so militant a power that the only fitting way to speak of death is similar to the way one speaks of God. Death is the living power and presence in this world which feigns to be God."[19]

In his Letter to the Romans, St. Paul reminds us that after the fall of our first parents, "Death reigned" (Romans 5:14). The Greek word here for "reigned" is "lorded" or "ruled." We know this to be a fact. We can't escape Death.

Sin too reigns. Paul writes again, in Romans 3:9, that "all men, both Jews and Greeks, are under the power"—the rule, the lordship—"of sin." When he speaks of Sin like this, it's with a capital S! When we think of Sin, we tend to think of actions: something I did or didn't do, something I said or didn't say. But before sinful actions, Sin is a *power*. It exercises authority in the human race. Again, it's easy to prove this. Just ask yourself these questions: "Have you ever done something that you knew you shouldn't do, that you didn't want to do, or that you actually hated doing, but you did it anyway? Did you ever wonder why?" Because Sin is a power.

Paul, again in Romans, writes,

> For he who has died is freed from sin. But if we have died
> with Christ, we believe that we shall also live with him. For
> we know that Christ being raised from the dead will never die
> again; death no longer has dominion over him. (Romans 6:7-9)

Scripture speaks of Death and Sin as powers. Had Jesus
not done what He did through his death and resurrection, we
would still be subject to the powers of Sin and Death. You know
how, at a Baptism, we all think, "Oh, what a cute little child, so
innocent, so sweet"? Actually, in the reality of our biblical worldview, he's not. He's actually a child of darkness. What I mean
by that is he or she is born under the dominion—the rule, the
lordship—of Hell. That means there's no escape from Death or
enslavement to Sin for this child on his own. That's why we're
asking God to help us understand how hopeless we would be
if He hadn't done anything. God *has* done something (thank
God!), but one of the reasons we don't think of the gospel as
extraordinary news is because we don't know that the bad news
is not just bad, but it is our worst nightmare. We want to grasp
that, so that when we examine what Jesus has done for us, we
have a clear understanding of how we would be utterly hopeless apart from Him.

Here's St. Paul in Romans 7:15, 19-20:

> I do not understand my own actions. For I do not do what I
> want, but I do the very thing I hate. . . . For I do not do the
> good I want, but the evil I do not want is what I do. Now if I
> do what I do not want, it is no longer I that do it, but sin which
> dwells within me.

This is not just Paul talking about himself. He is talking about all human beings apart from the power of the Holy Spirit at work within their lives. Scott Hahn, in his *Commentary on Romans*, writes,

> The controlling metaphor of this section is slavery and freedom. Paul paints a black-or-white picture of the human situation: either one lives in service to sin and remains in spiritual bondage, or one lives in obedience to God and enjoys liberation from sin's captivity. It is a stark either-or: no fence-sitting, no third option.[20]

Notice that this is the opposite of how the world tends to think about the gospel and the Christian life—as full of restriction and limitation. In fact, the Christian life grants freedom. It is the avoidance of a Christian life that keeps us bound in slavery.

Here's how Fleming Rutledge put it:

> No one is capable of being captain of his own soul, master of her own fate. Each of us is worked upon by unconscious impulses of which we are not even aware and over which we have little control. Paul, unlike the typical American, does not think in terms of autonomous human beings. . . . *No one* is "free" in the domain of this world as it is. Either we must live our lives in the clutches of soul-destroying Powers or we are delivered into "the obedience of faith." [21]

The clear implication here is that the domain of Sin leads to Death; its goal as well as its purpose is Death. There is no way out of this downward-moving spiral of dissolution.

That's why God tells us in the Scriptures that we have two choices: life and death. Obedience, simply listening to our good Father, leads to life. Disobedience, listening to the enemy, leads to Death.

There is no way, on our own, for human beings to move from the domain of Sin to God's domain of righteousness. It requires an invasion of the kingdom of Sin from the outside. Why is that so important? Because it's not enough just to repent. We need Someone to rescue us from the slavery in which the human race finds itself with regards to Sin and Death. The domain of Sin leads to Death. That is its goal and purpose.

> Through the devil's envy death entered the world,
> and those who belong to his party experience it. (Wisdom 2:24)

Who is in his possession? The human race, unless we're in the hands of God.

Let me share with you the most powerful image I can imagine, especially for women (but this works for men too) for how to pray about this.

Arguably, other than abortion, the most horrific scourge on our planet right now is human trafficking. There are more slaves right now than there have been in the history of the world—both economic and sexual slaves. The most powerful way to understand our spiritual enslavement to Sin and Death is to imagine what it would be like to be abducted and enslaved.

I challenge you, at some point, to ask the Holy Spirit to help you enter into a meditation on this. Know that this exercise is not meant to draw you into darkness! Always be mindful that God *has* done something about our situation. He is our hope!

When you're ready to meditate on this, ask the Holy Spirit to help you imagine and understand what it would be like to have been captured, hidden away, and enslaved by a trafficker. Imagine that no one knows where you are, and that no one is coming for you. You're in the hands of someone who lives to use, harm, and degrade you. There's no way out. This will be your life now. Forever.

That's the situation of our race apart from God.

Breaking Out of the Prison

It is only because Someone *has* done something about our situation that the gospel is such extraordinary news. When you pray with this kind of imagery (and for men, I sometimes suggest trying to imagine captivity in a concentration camp or a prison), you can *feel* the despair of being captured. Such meditation takes you to a place that is utterly beyond hope. It takes you to the *grace* of despair: understanding the hopelessness of our situation apart from God.

But take heart, my friends. God doesn't want us to despair. He *has* done something for us. A rescue mission is coming, and Jesus is going to burst into that place of captivity and bring hope.

This chapter has been all about God exposing the enemy and shining a brilliant, cleansing light on the enemy's actions, as well as into your life personally. Ask the Holy Spirit to help you name the answers to the following questions:

- Where is the enemy accusing me right now?
- What lie is crippling me right now?
- Where is he causing division in my life?
- Where is he flattering my ego?
- What temptation is strongest in my life?
- Where am I most discouraged right now?

I encourage you to not only think about the answers to these questions but to also write them down. When you write them down, you *capture* them, and then you can move against them.

If we ask God to reveal these things, He will. Why? Because He's a good Father, and His desire is for His children to live in a good place. He doesn't want us to remain in captivity, and He knows precisely what to do.

Summary of Part II: Captured

- Scripture is "game film"—it equips us and tells us both "what happened" and "what will always happen."
- God is all good, but one of the creatures He made chose to rebel against God and us. That creature is the enemy, Satan.
- Satan, or the devil, is not an equal rival of God. He is merely a creature.
- The enemy's motive for rebellion was envy of the human race. He hates us and has declared war on us.

- His strategy: to convince us that God is not our loving Father and that we can be happy without God.
- His tactics: to accuse, lie, divide, flatter, tempt, and discourage.
- His goal: to destroy our lives.
- Because of Adam and Eve's free choice to believe Satan's lies (the fall), we are bound by the powers of Death and Sin.
- The grace of despair helps us see how dire our situation is: that we have literally been captured and are in need of rescue.

Discussion Questions

1. Do I believe that there really is an enemy who has a plan to ruin my life?
2. How do I see Satan differently after reading this chapter? How do I view the fall differently?
3. What lies and accusations has the enemy spoken into my life?
4. Ask Jesus to expose the lies, accusations, and divisions that the enemy has used or is using to wreak havoc in your life. Consider capturing those lies and accusations in writing. Ask God for the grace to hear His loving voice, not the hateful whispers of the enemy.

PART III

Rescued

As you read Part III, "Rescued," ask for the grace of unshakable confidence in Jesus as Lord of heaven and earth.

CHAPTER 9

Unshakable Confidence

God rest ye merry gentlemen
Let nothing you dismay
For Jesus Christ our Saviour
Was born on Christmas Day
To save us all from Satan's pow'r
When we were gone astray
O tidings of comfort and joy
—**Traditional English Carol**

We ended the last chapter asking the Holy Spirit to help us understand the utter hopelessness of being enslaved by a human trafficker. Let's ask the Holy Spirit to continue His work in our minds and hearts so that we might grasp better who Jesus is and what He has done to free us.

Imagine being in that room: bound, helpless, terrified. You want to sleep, but sleep is dangerous because it makes you even more vulnerable. So there's no rest. Suddenly you feel a hand on your shoulder. You jolt because, right now, touch means harm. But when you open your eyes, you see the face of a man who instantly puts you at ease. How did he get into this room? His face is warm and gentle, but there is something even more than mere gentleness about him. He exudes utter strength and confidence. Just the sight of him gives you a sense of security and the belief that this nightmare can end.

The man helps you to your feet, unties your hands, and tenderly brushes dust and debris from your shoulders. He is looking at you, calming you, and filling you with unspeakable hope. He walks you toward the locked door, outside of which your captor lurks. Conflicting emotions fight within: you fear the man who is outside, but you're exhilarated at the prospect of escaping this hellish place. As the man begins to turn the doorknob, you realize how much you dread—and don't want to witness—the confrontation between this gentle man and the fiend outside.

But as you leave the room, it becomes clear that the confrontation has already taken place. The trafficker is on the floor, hands and feet bound, mouth covered with duct tape. He cannot touch you. As you step around the one who terrorized you, the man who bound your tormentor turns to you and, with a smile so radiant you can hardly bear it, says, "He can't harm you now. I have overcome him. I sought you out and rescued you from his grip. Do not be afraid anymore."

This is the best way I know to enter into this chapter, which focuses our attention on the extraordinary response of God to the situation of our race. What has He done about the hopeless predicament we were in? God has rescued us. He didn't send an angel, teach us a new method, or start a new program. *God Himself* has rescued us, and in a most spectacular way.

The following passage from Isaiah can better help us enter into this incredible story of God's rescue of our race:

> Can the prey be taken from the mighty,
>   or the captives of a tyrant be rescued?
> Surely, thus says the LORD:
> "Even the captives of the mighty shall be taken,
>   and the prey of the tyrant shall be rescued,
> for I will contend with those who contend with you. . . .
> Then all flesh shall know
>   that I am the LORD your Savior,
>   and your Redeemer, the Mighty One of Jacob."
> (Isaiah 49:24-25, 26)

"Can the prey be taken from the mighty?" God answers with a resounding yes and says that He Himself will contend with those who contend with us. This is a promise!

He does this because He is the "LORD your Savior, and your Redeemer." Let's pause a moment to understand the word "redeemer." The Hebrew word for "redeemer" is *goel*. In ancient Israel, *goel* referred to the male family member who had an obligation to act on behalf of his relatives if certain things happened. For example, if a family member was sold or sold himself into slavery, the *goel* had the obligation to buy the person back from captivity. Or if a relative was murdered, the *goel's* obligation was to avenge that death. With this in mind, note what God says in Isaiah! The God who made a universe that is ninety-plus billion light years across considers you and me His *family*. Jesus fights against and destroys the power of Death, thus avenging and liberating us from the tyranny of Sin.

Before we explore further, let me offer one more helpful image. The great Russian iconographer Andrei Rublev created an icon, *The Trinity,* that depicts three figures seated around a table. They are the three heavenly messengers sent to Abraham in Genesis 18. The visitors tell him and his wife, Sarah, that they're going to have a child, Isaac, who will be the heir to the covenant God has made with Abraham. (When you get a moment, try to find the image online so you can pray with it.)

I once came across an interpretation of this icon as a depiction of a conversation taking place within the Trinity after the rebellion of Adam in the garden. The figure on the left is the Father, the One in the middle is the Son, and the One on the right is the Holy Spirit. The Father, the interpretation goes, looks to the other Persons of the Trinity and poses these questions: "Who will go and get him? Who will bring him back? Who will bring him home?" The Son has His head turned towards the Father to say, "I will! I will go and get him. I will bring him home." And the Spirit has His head turned down, for He knows what it will cost the Son to do this: His life.

I invite you to enter into that scene in prayer and understand that the "him" or "her" the Trinity is talking about is *you*. God will not let His children remain in the hands of the enemy. As one author said, you are far more important than you ever dared to imagine! As we enter more deeply into this theme, I desire to lift Jesus up in a way that perhaps will be new for many of you, especially men. My experience as a priest is that many people think of Jesus as kind, gentle, compassionate, meek, mild, merciful, and loving. He is all of these and more, to be sure! But Jesus is not *only* these things. Jesus is also utterly unconquerable. He is *Lord*, which isn't just a conclusion to our prayers. It is who He is. And because of this, the grace we want to pray for in this chapter is unshakable confidence in God.

As with the other parts of this book, there is far too much to cover here. Years could be devoted to what I am going to merely touch on. But I hope this condensed version will help us better understand what God has done for us and will give us a new way of looking at Jesus.

We will look at three questions in this part of the book:

- Why did Jesus come?
- What was Jesus doing on the cross?
- What difference does this make?

CHAPTER 10

Why Did Jesus Come?

What is the life of Jesus all about? Did He come merely to tell stories, to exhort us to be kind and love one another, to perform a few miracles, and then to meet a tragic, premature end? He did all these things, to be sure, but these aren't the reasons He came.

Let's recall the imagery of the Allies landing on D-Day: the landing crafts hitting the beach, the doors opening, soldiers pouring out, warriors storming the beaches. "Why have they landed?" we asked. They landed to fight, to go to war, and to liberate a people in the hands of a tyrant.

Why did God enter into His creation and land as a man? The answer is the same. God became man to fight, to go to war, to liberate an oppressed race, and to free prisoners. He invaded an enslaved world to rescue the creature that means the most to Him—not just generic "humanity," but *you*, personally. Yes, *you*, the person He knows by name. Scripture tells us this repeatedly, but we don't always know Scripture as well as we'd like. This is why it's vital to soak ourselves in God's word and absorb these truths. Scripture is bursting with the truths God wants to communicate that we don't otherwise hear enough of. Let's look at a few passages that help us understand the answer to this first question and what God is revealing to us in His word.

In the most succinct summary I know, 1 John 3:8 tells us the purpose behind the Incarnation—that is, God becoming flesh in the womb of the Virgin Mary—"The reason the Son of God appeared was to destroy the works of the devil." It doesn't get any clearer than this, folks!

At the start of Jesus' public ministry, as recorded in Luke chapter 4, He gives what is often referred to as his "inaugural address." Just as at the start of his term, a politician offers a glimpse into what he or she hopes to accomplish, so Jesus does in the synagogue in Nazareth. Luke tells us that Jesus stood up to read the Scriptures and opened the scroll to the section of Isaiah where the prophet says,

> The Spirit of the Lord is upon me,
> because he has anointed me to preach good news
>   to the poor.
> He has sent me to proclaim release to the captives
> and recovering of sight to the blind,
> to set at liberty those who are oppressed,
> to proclaim the acceptable year of the Lord. (4:18-19)

After reading this, Jesus tells the crowd, "Today, this scripture has been fulfilled in your hearing" (Luke 4:21). Who are these "captives" Jesus is speaking about? Who are the oppressed, and what is oppressing them? The captives are the entire race of men and women, oppressed by the powers of Sin and Death and Satan.

The Gospel of Mark gives us a different start to the public ministry of Jesus. Mark 1 records an encounter between Jesus and a demon-possessed man in the synagogue in Capernaum. The demon cries out, "What have you to do with us, Jesus of Nazareth? Have you come to destroy us?" (Mark 1:24). The answer is clear in Jesus' immediate action: He drives the demon out of the man. But note how this happens. We don't see a massive struggle between Jesus and the demon. In fact, there's no struggle at all! Jesus simply addresses the demon and says, "Be silent" (1:25). The Greek word Mark used can be understood as "Be muzzled." Picture that! A man is shrieking at Jesus, utterly out of control because he's possessed by an unclean spirit, and Jesus almost casually says, "Hush up. Quiet. Stop talking. Be muzzled." He vanquishes a demon as easily as you and I would swat a fly. He rescues the man from the grip of the demon, displaying for all His superiority over the powers of darkness.

The Gospel of Luke records another encounter between Jesus and a demon-possessed man. Just as in the Gospel of Mark, Jesus drives out the demon and rescues the man from its grip. Immediately, the religious leaders accuse Jesus of driving out the demon by the power of the devil. Jesus tells them this is absurd. "If Satan also is divided against himself," He asks, "how will his kingdom stand?" (Luke 11:18). He then offers a parable that is paramount for understanding why He came: "When a strong man, fully armed, guards his own palace, his goods are in peace" (11:21).

Let's pause to make sure we grasp what the Lord is telling us. Who is this "strong man?" None other than Satan, the enemy of our race. And what is "his own palace?" His palace is our world (remember how Jesus identifies Satan as the "ruler of this world" in John 12:31). Finally, what are "his goods"? That would be us—the entire human race—which has sold itself into slavery by our rebellion against God in the garden at the dawn of our history.

Jesus continues this parable. "But," He says, "when one stronger than he assails him and overcomes him, he takes away his armor in which he trusted, and divides his spoil" (Luke 11:22). Jesus is clear: not only is He stronger than the "strong man," but He has come to attack and overcome the strong man.

In other words, Jesus has come to fight. And the result of His attacking and overcoming the strong man is that His possessions—that is, *us*—are no longer bound and can go free.

In the Gospel of John, shortly before Jesus enters into His Passion, He explains what He is about to do: "*Now* is the judgment of this world, now shall the ruler of this world be cast out" (12:31, emphasis mine). The same theme we saw in the parable is found here. Jesus will cast out the creature that has held our race bound.

Vanquishing evil is what Jesus came to do. His authority in commanding unclean spirits prompted wonder and amazement in the people. And yet today, all too often, the way we talk about Jesus provokes little wonder and amazement. Peter Kreeft, philosophy professor at Boston College, said that we, as Christians, have tragically managed to undo the miracle of Cana. Remember that miracle, when Jesus turned 180 gallons of water into wine? Kreeft says that contemporary Christians have turned the wine back into water. We have somehow managed to turn the only person who never bored anybody into someone boring.

I can't speak for you, but as a student for years in Catholic schools, Jesus wasn't always presented as Someone a young man would want to follow. How many of us endured religious education classes in which we made collages or some other silly thing? The *power* of Jesus was not presented. Jesus walked on water; fed five thousand men with a couple of loaves of bread; and made blind people see, deaf people hear, and lame people walk. He was a man who, at least three times, called the dead back to life!

Frank Sheed, an English apologist in the last century, remarked once that the people who followed Jesus (prostitutes, tax collectors, and other "sinners") were people who were easily bored, who thought life was about sex, money, or simply living for themselves . . . *until* they met Jesus. When they encountered Him, they abandoned their pursuit of pleasure, wealth, or selfishness. They came to understand that a truly rich life was one that revolved around Him. In short, when contemporaries of Jesus met Him, they had one of two radical responses: they either dropped everything and followed Him, or they demanded, "Kill Him!" No one ever yawned, shrugged, and said, "Meh. Nothing to see here." The constant response of the crowds was shock and awe.

The answer to our first question—*Why did Jesus come?*—is further expounded on in the Gospel of Luke. Those of us who pray the Liturgy of the Hours (which all priests and deacons promise to pray daily) recite this passage every morning:

Blessed be the Lord God of Israel:
he has come to his people and set them free.
He has raised up for us a mighty savior,
born of the house of his servant David.

Through his holy prophets he promised of old
that he would save us from our enemies,
from the hands of all who hate us.

He promised to show mercy to our fathers
and to remember his holy covenant.

This was the oath He swore to our father Abraham:
to set us free from the hands of our enemies,
free to worship him without fear,
holy and righteous in his sight all the days of our life.

You, my child, shall be called the prophet of the Most High;
for you will go before the Lord to prepare his way,
to give his people knowledge of salvation
by the forgiveness of their sins.

In the tender compassion of our God
the dawn from on high shall break upon us,
to shine on those who dwell in darkness and the shadow of death,
and to guide our feet into the way of peace.[22]

Note the repeated theme: "He has *come*," "set them *free*,"
"a mighty *Savior*," "*save us* from our *enemies*," and "from the
hands of *all who hate us.*"

Who are these "enemies"? Not a political party or some other race or sex, not the football team you can't stand or a country you fear. These are not our enemies. Our enemies are Sin, Death, Hell, and Satan. And who dwells in darkness and the shadow of death? We do. We live haunted daily by Death. Only God can guide us to the way of peace. And He does!

Our cozy images of "little Jesus, meek and mild" were never really accurate. Jesus is a warrior. *The* warrior. The Book of Wisdom says this:

> While gentle silence enveloped all things,
> and night in its swift course was now half gone,
> your all-powerful word leaped from heaven, from the
>   royal throne,
> into the midst of a land doomed,
> a stern warrior. (Wisdom 18:14-15, NRSVCE)

Just as the troops showed up on D-Day to fight, Jesus landed to march into battle. God becoming man is the invasion of one kingdom (darkness, Hell, Death, Sin, and Satan) by a stronger kingdom—the kingdom of God. But He invaded in a most clever fashion. God, as a man, stepped onto the stage of human history to trick and fight the one who tricked us into selling ourselves into slavery. C. S. Lewis put it this way: "Christianity is the story of how the rightful king has landed, you might say landed in disguise."[23]

Jesus came to fight.

CHAPTER 11

What Was Jesus Doing on the Cross?

Before you read this next section, find a crucifix, and take a few moments to look at Jesus there. As you do, ask yourself these questions: "Does this look like a warrior? Is Jesus on the cross the hunted? Or is He the hunter? Is He the victim or is He the aggressor?"

At first glance, the answers to these questions seem obvious. A man is nailed on a cross. He's crowned with thorns, His body streaked with His own blood from the terrible scourging He has endured. He has a gaping wound in His side. Crucifixion, deliberately done in the middle of a major intersection so that *everyone* would see it, was the ancient world's most humiliating and degrading way to kill someone. Everyone was invited to this free-for-all public spectacle, and it was a warning from the Romans: "This will happen to you if you dare mess with us." And despite the design of those crucifixes in our churches, the man on this cross was stark naked.

Clearly, on the cross, Jesus looks like the hunted, the victim, and anything but a warrior. But remember who Jesus is. This isn't merely a man; this is God made man. This is the One through whom and for whom everything that is seen and unseen was created. This is the One through whom a universe that is ninety-plus billion light years across was made! How could anyone possibly nail *God* to a cross? Where do you get that kind of nail? Jesus says shortly before He enters into His Passion, "*No one* takes [my life] from me" (John 10:18, emphasis mine). Just a little later, He goes on to say, "The ruler of this world is coming. *He has no power over me*" (14:30, emphasis mine).

In short, there's only one way that God can be nailed to a cross: He has to want it to happen. But why?

There are three ways of answering that question. Each is a legitimate answer, with roots found both in Sacred Scripture and the teaching of the Church. Not one of the ways, however, is an exhaustive explanation; they must all be held together. The three explanations for what Jesus is doing on the cross are:

- Jesus is showing us the love of the Father.
- Jesus is making atonement for us.
- Jesus is going to war to rescue us.

When I was growing up in the seventies, I remember hearing only about the first explanation. "God is love" was the constant refrain. And to be sure, He is! As for atonement, most people understand that Jesus' sacrifice has something to do with our Sin. But very few people have ever thought about Jesus as a warrior on the cross fighting on our behalf. So let's unpack these three ways of understanding what Jesus was doing.

First, Jesus on the cross *is* showing us how great the Father's love is. John 3:16 says it all: "For God so loved the world that he gave his only Son, that whoever believes in him should not perish but have eternal life." This message comes through again and again in Scripture. St. Paul says, "God shows his love for us in that while we were yet sinners Christ died for us" (Romans 5:8) and

> God, who is rich in mercy, out of the great love with which he loved us, even when we were dead through our trespasses, made us alive together with Christ (by grace you have been saved), and raised us up with him, and made us sit with him in the heavenly places in Christ Jesus, that in the coming ages he might show the immeasurable riches of his grace in kindness toward us in Christ Jesus. (Ephesians 2:4-7)

The First Letter of John reminds us, "See what love the Father has given us, that we should be called children of God; and so we are" (3:1). Later in that same letter he writes,

> In this the love of God was made manifest among us, that God sent his only Son into the world, so that we might live through him. In this is love, not that we have loved God, but that he loved us and sent his Son to be the expiation for our sins. (4:9-10)

So Jesus is definitely showing us the love of the Father. But that's not all He's doing. The passage from 1 John 4:10 transitions us to the second explanation: that Jesus was making atonement ("expiation") for our sins. The root of the word "expiation" is found in the Old Testament and refers to a sacrifice offered to God to expiate, or remove, something that has created a distance between us and God. John helps us understand that Jesus on the cross was restoring our relationship with God—a relationship that was broken because of our sins. Earlier in 1 John, he writes that Jesus "is the expiation for our sins, and not for ours only but also for the sins of the whole world" (2:2). The Letter to the Hebrews continues this theme when it says,

> Therefore [Jesus] had to be made like his brethren in every respect, so that he might become a merciful and faithful high priest in the service of God, to make expiation for the sins of the people. (2:17)

While this language is unfamiliar to some of us, we are probably familiar with John the Baptist's cry, "Behold, the Lamb of God, who takes away the sin of the world!" (John 1:29). This understanding of Jesus also has its roots in the Old Testament, especially in connection with the exodus story, the deliverance of the Hebrew people from slavery.

On the night before the Hebrew people were dramatically rescued from their slavery (which foreshadows Jesus delivering the human race from slavery), they were instructed to take and slaughter a lamb, smear the lamb's blood on the lintels of their homes, and then eat the lamb's flesh in what is forever after known as the Passover meal. The lambs that were slaughtered were "types," or foreshadowings, of the blood of

Jesus that would be poured out on the cross for us and of His Body and Blood to be offered to us at every Mass we celebrate. The lamb also appears in the suffering servant songs of Isaiah, which are striking prophecies of the Lord's Passion:

Surely he has borne our griefs
    and carried our sorrows; . . .
But he was wounded for our transgressions,
    he was bruised for our iniquities;
upon him was the chastisement that made us whole,
    and with his stripes we are healed. (53:4, 5)

He was oppressed, and he was afflicted,
    yet he opened not his mouth;
like a lamb that is led to the slaughter,
    and like a sheep that before its shearers is silent,
    so he did not open his mouth. (53:7, NRSVCE)

There are countless passages that support this second way of understanding what Jesus was doing on the cross, but most striking is this passage from St. Paul: "For our sake [the Father] made him to be sin who knew no sin, so that in him we might become the righteousness of God" (2 Corinthians 5:21).

Through St. Paul, the Holy Spirit is telling us that Jesus on the cross was doing something to make us right with God. Jesus wasn't *passive*. This was, as Frank Sheed once remarked, the most *active* moment of Jesus' whole life.[24] He was willing to be there for you and me. The sinless One made His life a sacrifice to atone for all the sins of the entire human race, just as He told the apostles in the Upper Room during the Last

Supper that He would. There, after He had blessed, broken and distributed the bread to them, He took the chalice in His hands and likewise blessed it, saying, "Drink of it, all of you; for this is my blood of the covenant, which is poured out for many for the forgiveness of sins" (Matthew 26:27-28). This was in keeping with what the angel told Joseph after Mary had virginally conceived: "You shall call his name Jesus, for he will save his people from their sins" (1:21).

Have you seen the movie *The Passion of the Christ*? I remember the first time I saw the scourging scene. In Scripture, there's one simple sentence: "Then Pilate took Jesus and scourged him" (John 19:1). For the biblical audience at that time, one sentence was enough. They *knew* what scourging was. We don't, and so the movie shows us. It forces us to look at the horror of scourging and shows us what God endured to make atonement for us.

So we watch this man—this *God-man*—get ripped to shreds. Those whose job it was to scourge were trained to do it in such a way that they brought the person to the brink of death without killing him. It was an "art." They were usually drunk when they did it because what they were doing to another human being was so repulsive and horrific. At the end of a wooden handle with leather strips were little pieces of bone or metal, designed to embed into the flesh—to rip it off. These would get into nerves and tendons and rip them out. They scourged the prisoner until he was almost dead, but not quite, because they wanted him to be alive when he was crucified.

When I first watched that scourging scene in *The Passion*, I started crying. I kept saying out loud, over and over, "Oh God, I am *so sorry* for all the sins I committed without a second thought. I'm sorry for everything that I thought at the time was no big deal. And *this* is the price You paid to make me right with You. Oh God, *forgive me*."

We simply have not understood the seriousness of Sin. Jesus on the cross has *become Sin* so that we could become the righteousness of God. But as true as this understanding is, I don't think it moves many people. Most of us have an unrealistic sense of our own sinfulness. Most of us, when we look at the cross, think, "I'm not *that* bad of a guy, not *that* sinful, not to the point that He had to do *that*." The truth is that we *are* in need of the extreme remedy that is the crucifixion of the Son of God.

Finally, what about the third way of understanding what Jesus was doing on the cross: going to war to rescue us? Let me share an experience I had several years ago that has forever changed how I look at Jesus on the cross. Just before Holy Week, I was in my chapel praying, pondering the Scriptures for the great events we were about to celebrate, when I suddenly, distinctly, and out of nowhere heard two words that I had never heard together before in my life. I have learned that God often "speaks" through inspirations and images and things of that sort, and this felt like the Holy Spirit had mysteriously put a new expression into my mind.

Ambush predator.

I thought, *What the heck is an "ambush predator"?* I pulled out my phone and googled it. Images popped up: snakes, spiders, and ocean creatures I had never seen before. These creatures live in the woods, the desert, in water, even in our houses! I started to laugh out loud. *Ambush predator*, I discovered, is a term used for various creatures that lie motionless and still, camouflaged in their environments, for one purpose: to attract the prey. And when the prey gets close? They pounce. As I began praying with this, I lingered over the Lord's final hours before He died, starting with His time in the Garden of Gethsemane. It's as if, from the moment when Jesus began to sweat blood, His divinity was more and more "cloaked," or camouflaged.

Certainly, with the exception of the Transfiguration, when Jesus let Peter, James, and John briefly see His divinity burst forth in that brilliant light, His divinity was never fully on display (although glimpses of His power and majesty were displayed in the many miracles He performed). But from the agony in the garden until He dies on the cross, He looks like not only a mere man but a man who is utterly helpless as He is arrested, chained, and slapped. Pause for a moment with me. The God who made the universe that's ninety-plus billion light years across *allows* Himself to be slapped. The judge of heaven and earth *allows* Himself to be judged by Pilate. He's stripped naked, scourged until He is teetering on the brink of death, and then crowned with thorns. Finally, He is nailed to a cross. Why? To attract His prey.

Jesus on the cross is *the* Ambush Predator. While He is definitely showing us the Father's great love and of course is making atonement for our sins, He is also drawing the enemy close. He is drawing Satan, enticing Death to Himself. Why? So that He can bind the strong man and destroy Death from inside.

God became a man to fight, to rescue us, to get His creation—*you*—back. He landed on earth in order to vanquish the enemy, but here's the challenge: the enemy won't fight God. Satan isn't stupid. Satan knew he couldn't beat God and wouldn't try, so God designed a plan: a plan He knew would involve piercing, nails, and a cross. Then He hid Himself as a man. And He waited.

When I pray with this idea, I find it helpful to approach it imaginatively (in the way that St. Ignatius encouraged us to "see" Scripture as we pray with it). Picture the scene: Jesus is hanging on the cross, naked, bloody, and physically weakened beyond belief. He is crowned with thorns and nailed to a piece of wood, in tremendous pain. I imagine the enemy coming close to Him, standing in front of Him. Satan begins to taunt Jesus, saying something like "Y'know, You're a rather interesting character. You do some pretty astounding miracles, but . . . (I imagine the devil sneering at this point) . . . I don't see any miracles now." Then I imagine Satan looking at his watch, maybe even yawning, and saying, "And You know what? In a few minutes, You're *mine*. Because *nobody* escapes Death. *I* will have You."

And that's exactly what Jesus wants. The Ambush Predator has drawn the prey. He will enter into Death and, from the inside, destroy its power. Jesus on the cross is not the poor, helpless victim, and He is not the hunted. Jesus on the cross is the aggressor and the hunter.

This sounds beyond strange to most of us. But this is not just my own fanciful imagination. This was a frequent way that the early Church preached about Jesus's work on the cross. In an Easter sermon given by St. Ephrem, a fourth-century deacon and the only Syrian Doctor of the Church, we find these words:

> Death trampled our Lord underfoot, but he in his turn treated death as a highroad for his own feet. He submitted to it, enduring it willingly, because by this means he would be able to

destroy death in spite of itself. Death had its own way when our Lord went out from Jerusalem carrying his cross; but when by a loud cry from that cross he summoned the dead from the underworld, death was powerless to prevent it.

Death slew him by means of the body which he had assumed, but that same body proved to be the weapon with which he conquered death. Concealed beneath the cloak of his manhood, his godhead engaged death in combat; but in slaying our Lord, death itself was slain. It was able to kill natural human life, but was itself killed by the life that is above the nature of man.

Death could not devour our Lord unless he possessed a body, neither could hell swallow him up unless he bore our flesh; and so he came in search of a chariot in which to ride to the underworld. This chariot was the body which he received from the Virgin; in it he invaded death's fortress, broke open its strongroom and scattered all its treasure.[25]

Imagine the power of hearing that homily! Here is Jesus the warrior, fighting for us, binding the strong man and setting us free!

Here's another sermon from the early Church, proclaimed by Maximus the Confessor in the seventh century:

His flesh was set before that voracious, gaping dragon as bait to provoke him: flesh that would be deadly for the dragon, for it would utterly destroy him by the power of the Godhead hidden within it. For human nature, however, his flesh was to be a remedy since the power of the Godhead in it would restore human nature to its original grace.

Just as the devil had poisoned the tree of knowledge and spoiled our nature by its taste, so too, in presuming to devour the Lord's flesh he himself is corrupted and is completely destroyed by the power of the Godhead hidden in it.[26]

St. Irenaeus, another hero of the early Church, martyred in Lyon in the early third century, wrote this:

[Christ has] summed up all things, both waging war against our enemy, and crushing him who had at the beginning led us away captives in Adam, and trampled upon his head.[27]

Melito of Sardis, preaching on Easter in the early second century, gave a sermon that I often refer to as "the trash-talking Jesus." He preaches as if Jesus is speaking, carrying over this same theme we are talking about here:

The Lord clothed himself with humanity, and with suffering on behalf of the suffering one, and bound on behalf of the one constrained, and judged on behalf of the one convicted, and buried on behalf of the one entombed, he rose from the dead and cried out aloud: "Who takes issue with me? Let him stand before me. I set free the condemned. I gave life to the dead. I raise up the entombed. Who will contradict me?"

"It is I," says the Christ, "I am he who destroys death, and triumphs over the enemy, and crushes Hades, and binds the strong man, and bears humanity off to the heavenly heights. It is I," says the Christ.
"So come all families of people, adulterated with sin, and receive forgiveness of sins. For I am your freedom. I am the Passover

of salvation, I am the lamb slaughtered for you, I am your ransom, I am your life, I am your light, I am your salvation, I am your resurrection, I am your King. I shall raise you up by my right hand, I will lead you to the heights of heaven, there shall I show you the everlasting Father."

He it is who made the heaven and the earth, and formed humanity in the beginning, who was proclaimed through the law and the prophets, who took flesh from a virgin, who was hung on a tree, who was buried in earth, who was raised from the dead, and ascended to the heights of heaven, who sits at the right hand of the Father, who has the power to save all things, through whom the Father acted from the beginning and for ever.

This is the alpha and omega, this is the beginning and the end, the ineffable beginning and the incomprehensible end. This is the Christ, this is the King, this is Jesus, this is the commander, this is the Lord, this is he who rose from the dead, this is he who sits at the right hand of the Father, he bears the Father and is borne by him. To him be the glory and the might for ever. Amen.[28]

As I have discovered, the Church Fathers (those men who preached, wrote, and taught in the first few centuries after Jesus' ascension), such as Augustine, Gregory of Nyssa, Justin Martyr, Origen, and others, often spoke of God becoming man so as to do battle against the devil. Gregory explains Jesus' action on the cross with the analogy of a fish hook and bait (the bait being His humanity, and the hook, His divinity). Augustine uses the imagery of a mousetrap, with His flesh being the lure, and His divinity, the means by which the prey is caught. Both men point out how fitting it is that the one who deceived our race at its beginning should himself be deceived by God into bringing about the ruin of his own kingdom.

One of the most creative ways this has been displayed is in a strange scene in *The Passion of the Christ*. Just after Jesus dies, we get a view of the cross from high above, where a drop of water forms and then falls to the ground, symbolizing the tears of heaven as Jesus offers up His life for us. Immediately after this is a bizarre scene that shows Satan standing on dry, barren earth, shrieking. It's not a cry of victory, but one of being anguished and stunned and one of utter defeat. Mel Gibson captured on film what Augustine, Gregory, Maximus, Ephrem, and so many other early Church Fathers had preached: Jesus on the cross went to war and crushed Satan's power.

This interpretation of Jesus' work helps us understand what Jesus meant when He uttered His cry from the cross: "It is finished" (John 19:30). What was Jesus saying? Not, "Phew, that's finally over." It's a victory cry by our Lord. The word "finished" can also be interpreted as *accomplished, fulfilled, carried out, performed, achieved*, or *completed*. He came to rescue us, to set us free, to bind the strong man. And by His death and resurrection, the Ambush Predator has done it.[29]

CHAPTER 12

What Difference Does It Make?

We come now to the final part of this section. In the words of a friend of mine, "So? *Now* what?" What difference does any of this make in our lives?

It changes *everything*!

By his death and glorious resurrection from the dead, Jesus has

- humiliated the enemy,
- destroyed Death,
- transferred us,
- given us access to the Father,
- recreated us,
- rendered Sin impotent,
- given us authority over the enemy, and
- sent us on a mission to get His world back.

Let's mine these riches one at a time, the first four in this chapter and the next four in the following chapter.

The First Difference: Jesus Has Humiliated the Enemy

This point is a favorite of mine. In Colossians 2:15, Paul writes, "He disarmed the principalities and powers and made a public example of them, triumphing over them in him." Let's translate that literally: *Jesus stripped and disrobed the powers of Death, Sin, Satan, and Hell, utterly humiliated them, and triumphed over them.*

The word "triumph" has become diluted, but in Paul's day, everyone understood exactly what it meant.

In the early Roman Empire, a triumph was a megaparade—a spectacle to end all spectacles. Triumphs took place in the city of Rome to celebrate monumental victories by a military leader. In the later years of the empire, they were reserved only for the Roman emperor. Triumphs were all-day events that began with the victor giving a speech to the Senate and all the people of Rome. The people would honor and praise him for his accomplishment, he would dress in special robes, and then he would step into his chariot and begin a procession that started at the Porta Triumphalis (Gate of Triumph), a gate into Rome that was reserved only for this purpose. The procession included a variety of people and politicians, as well as a sampling of those whom the military leader or emperor had captured. The prisoners were usually theatrically chained up.

The most moving image I've ever seen of this was a depiction of an event from the life of Julius Caesar. He had engaged in an eight-year battle with the king of Gaul and had finally defeated him. After his victory, Caesar's army apprehended the king of Gaul and brought him to Caesar, who was surrounded by his soldiers. As the king of Gaul stood before Caesar, one of the Roman soldiers came forward and used a knife to cut the king's robes. The robes fell away, and he was completely naked. Another soldier pushed him to the ground, on his knees, and another brought out the emblem of the Roman Empire, a golden eagle. They thrust it before his lips to make him kiss it, as if to say, "*You* have lost."

Then they stood him up and chained his hands behind his back. They put him in a cage and began the parade back to Rome. That was just the beginning of the triumph.

They marched for days, finally entered Rome, and made their way down the main street that led to the forum. We can picture Caesar in his chariot, fresh from the fields of victory, surrounded by his army and decked out in his regalia. The whole Roman Empire was in the streets to greet their victorious hero, a long line of captives behind him. At the very end of the line was a cage with a man in it—naked and chained, with a sign above his head that read, "This is the one who used to threaten and tyrannize us. He won't do that anymore."

Paul tells us that this is what Jesus has done to our enemy, Satan. He has *triumphed* over him and his "children"—the powers of Sin and Death. Satan has no more power over us. We don't need to be afraid of him.

It's important to clarify that while the ultimate battle has been won, we are still very much in a fight. Every day the enemy tries to deceive us, tempt us, and prevent us from reaching the goal for which God created us: to be divinized. Ronald Knox, a great English pastor in the early twentieth century, reminded people that what Jesus accomplished for us by His death and resurrection was not some sort of "all clear." Rather, it was the announcement that now we have a chance at victory since the principalities and powers have been defeated. This is why Peter warns us, "Be sober, be watchful. Your adversary the devil prowls around like a roaring lion, seeking some one to devour" (1 Peter 5:8). It's also why the Book of Revelation likewise warns us, "Woe to you, O earth and sea, for the devil has come down to you in great wrath, because he knows that his time is short!" (12:12). Note that last part: "He *knows* that his time is short." The devil knows he has lost, no matter how dire daily life looks.

The Second Difference: Jesus Has Destroyed the Power of Death

As I write this, I'm looking at a picture of my mom and dad, who have both passed away. My dad died as he left a college basketball game, collapsing after a heart attack in the arms of one of his grandsons. A few years later, Mom breathed her last in a hospital bed in her home, surrounded by her children. Like those of you who have lost loved ones, there's not a day that goes by when I don't think about them, miss them, and, more often than not, cry.

However, because of what Jesus has done on the cross, I can grieve with hope, as Paul encourages Christians to do (see 1 Thessalonians 4:13). Because the kingdom of Death can no longer hold one who belongs to Jesus, I do not fear for them, and I know I will see them if I stay close to the Lord myself until He comes for me. Death has lost its grip on the human race. Will I still die? Of course. So will you. But Death can't hold us anymore, thanks to what Jesus did on the cross.

This truth does not mean that we don't grieve. We grieve intensely. I miss greatly those I love who have departed the earth. Such grief is particularly painful for parents who have endured the trauma of burying a child. But I continually ask myself, and I encourage parents to ask, "Where are our lost loved ones?" If they're home with the Lord or on their way, the truth is that they don't miss anything here, as hard as it is for us to go on without them. A very thin veil exists between them and us, and the communion of saints means there is still a real exchange of love and friendship. Of the death of younger persons, I often hear people say, "What a tragedy!" For us, yes! But not for them. No one in heaven says, "Gosh, I feel cheated. If only I'd had a chance to drive a car or get married or see Tahiti." Heaven is not less than this life. It's infinitely more.

In Isaiah 25, God said through the prophet that he would do something about "the veil that is spread over all nations"—Death:

And he will destroy on this mountain the covering that is cast over all peoples, the veil that is spread over all nations. He will swallow up death for ever, and the Lord GOD will wipe away tears from all faces, and the reproach of his people he will take away from all the earth; for the LORD has spoken. (25:7-8)

This, my friends, is a promise! That promise is seen fulfilled in the Book of Revelation at the very end of history. There, the seer John writes,

And I heard a great voice from the throne saying, 'Behold, the dwelling of God is with men. He will dwell with them, and they shall be his people, and God himself will be with them; he will wipe every tear from their eyes, and death shall be no more, neither shall there be mourning nor crying nor pain any more, for the former things have passed away. (Revelation 21:3-4)

St. Paul, in a letter to his friend and protégé Timothy, says, "Our Savior Christ Jesus . . . *abolished* death and brought life and immortality to light through the gospel" (2 Timothy 1:10, emphasis mine). The Greek word that is translated as "abolished" into English can also mean: *wiped out, made powerless, exhausted, set aside, invalidated,* or *caused to become nothing.* This is what Jesus has done to the kingdom of Death!

In the Book of Revelation, when Jesus shows Himself to John, he says, "Fear not, I am the first and the last, and the living one; I died, and behold I am alive for evermore, and I have the keys of Death and Hades" (1:17-18). Who else do you know who can say these words? Only one person: Jesus! As one saint put it, "It is easier for [Jesus] to raise the dead to life than it is for us to rouse those who are sleeping."[30]

The result of Jesus destroying Death is that we have freedom. We are no longer bound by the fear of Death. The Letter to the

Hebrews says, "Since therefore the children share in flesh and blood, [Jesus] himself likewise partook of the same nature, that through death he might destroy him who has the power of death, that is, the devil, and deliver all those who *through fear of death were subject to lifelong bondage*" (2:14-15, emphasis mine).

Are you afraid of dying? I am not, and you don't have to be either. Death can't hold us. Will it take us one day? Absolutely, but it can't *hold* us. Death has no power over us because Jesus has risen from the dead. Or as Paul puts it, "Where, O death, is your victory? / Where, O death, is your sting? / . . . But thanks be to God, who gives us the victory through our Lord Jesus Christ" (1 Corinthians 15:55, 57, NRSVCE).

I can—and do—stand at the graves of my mother, my father, my brother, the graves of all those I love that I've buried, and I can taunt Death:

You. Do. Not. Win. You don't hold them, and you won't hold me.

I can say that, not because I am strong—I'm not—but because of what Jesus has done.

The Third Difference: Jesus Has Transferred Us to His Kingdom

Paul wrote about the *dominion* (government, rule, or authority) of darkness:

> He has delivered us from the dominion of darkness and transferred us to the kingdom of his beloved Son, in whom we have redemption, the forgiveness of sins. (Colossians 1:13-14)

God has transferred, or moved, us out of the kingdom of darkness and into *His* kingdom. If you are baptized, this happened in a real and literal way the moment you were baptized with water in the name of the Father, the Son, and the Holy Spirit.

As I mentioned in chapter 8, at birth we appear to be angelic little creatures, but the reality is that we're born as children of darkness because Adam and Eve unknowingly sold our race into slavery to powers against which we can't compete. It's as if the spiritual passport we're issued upon coming into this world says, "Belongs to the kingdom of darkness." We're born under the dominion and tyranny of Sin and Death; we are hopeless to escape their power *on our own*. (But not ultimately hopeless, thanks to Jesus.) This is *why* we baptize. Because at the moment of baptism, we *move!* We get a new passport—a new stamp, new documentation, a fresh start, and a whole new life in a new kingdom.

A dear friend of mine, a Baptist pastor, once offered a powerful way to think about what happens in baptism. Imagine—and this won't be too hard for some of us—growing up in a home that is utterly dysfunctional. Home, if you can call it that, is a place full of abuse—verbal, physical, and sexual. Because of this, you do everything you can to avoid being home. You get involved in every extracurricular activity, play every sport, and stay out as late as you can. You sneak in quietly because you don't want to wake anyone up. You know that if you do, plates might fly, quite literally. You live in this home for years.

But across the street lives this truly amazing family. You can't stand them because they're so happy. You hear them every night outside your window. The father is always there, playing with his kids, throwing a football or a baseball around, shooting hoops, laughing with and enjoying them. You can *hear* the incredible relationship between him and his children. You hear the opposite of everything that is your life. And you're jealous because you long for what they have—to be loved, to be known, to be safe. You've never felt those things, living as you do in such an ugly, horrible, and violent place.

Then, one day when you're home alone, you hear a knock. You go to the door, open it, and it's the dad from across the street. He looks directly at you, right into your eyes, as if he really sees you and knows you. And then he says, "Would you like to come live with us?" And you don't even pack. You just run. You race across the street, and you don't look back.

You've been adopted. It's the first day of a whole new life, and it feels like emerging from darkness into light.

That is what God has done for us. Baptism moves us from the kingdom of a tyrant into the home of our good Father. Scott Hahn puts it this way: "The recipient of baptism undergoes a death to the bondage of sin and is brought to life again by a reception of grace."[31] Fleming Rutledge builds on this as she describes this transfer:

> It takes hard mental work to enter Paul's thought-world and understand that [his words] do not describe a bondage to a harsh puritanical code imposed upon us by a tyrannical outside force. He means the opposite. The gospel of Christ means precisely *deliverance from* tyrannical outside forces into a realm of light and life.[32]

As I've gotten older, I've experienced this more and more. Before I genuinely surrendered my life to Jesus and personally experienced the power of the Holy Spirit at work in me, I lived in the kingdom of darkness. I was oppressed and taunted by all those lies and accusations I was accustomed to listening to. That's no longer the case. I now know I am a beloved child of my heavenly Father and that He delights in me. And this is true for you too, if you've been baptized.[33]

The Fourth Difference: Jesus Has Given Us Access to the Father

Most of us take this point for granted. Let me give you an image to help.

I've been fortunate to serve as pastor of two large parishes that had roughly three thousand families, or about ten to twelve thousand people. If you called the office and asked to meet with me on any given day, the answer was almost always no, unless it was a true emergency. My days were already committed to caring for people who had called weeks earlier and asked the same question. A priest in a large parish is much like a physician. Certain hours are set aside for emergencies, but otherwise you have to get in the queue. How often I wished I could bilocate!

With that in mind, let this simple but astonishing truth sink in: you and I can talk to *God* anytime we want! You might have to wait days or weeks to see a busy pastor or doctor, but you can approach and talk with God—the One who created all that is—anytime you want! God can "multilocate."

One more helpful image is to think of the concept of access. The idea behind this word is that of a letter of introduction or, even better, a person physically introducing us and bringing us to the person we are wanting and needing to see. In the business world, networking and industry connections can grant such helpful access. On the negative side, we've all heard of situations in which someone got a job because he "knows someone who knows someone." In the world, that can feel unfair. But Jesus grants fairness and access to all. He introduces us to the Father, allowing us to come into the heavenly courts and to the One who created all that is.

This is what Paul means in his Letter to the Ephesians when he writes, "Through [Jesus] we . . . have access in one Spirit to the Father" (2:18).

CHAPTER 13

What Difference Does It Make? (Continued)

We've already outlined four consequences of Jesus' death and resurrection. Let's look at four more, which are just as important.

The Fifth Difference: Jesus Has Recreated Us

If you've seen *The Passion of the Christ*, one of the scenes that likely brought you to tears is when Jesus meets His mother on the road to Calvary. He's carrying his cross down the Via Dolorosa, and Mary situates herself so that He can see her face and find comfort and love during this agonizing death march. We then see a flashback: Mary remembers the young Jesus playing, running, stumbling. She sprints to His side, making sure He hasn't hurt Himself. The scene shifts back to the present, and Mary again runs to Jesus just as He falls under the weight of the cross. "I'm here!" she cries to Him. And Jesus looks up at her, touches her face ever so gently despite His pain, and says, "Behold, Mother. I make all things new."

Those words are found in the Book of Revelation 21:5, as history comes to a close and as the new Jerusalem comes down from heaven "as a bride adorned for her husband" (21:2). They're uttered by the One who sat upon the throne, triumphantly rose from the dead, and who, by His resurrection, began recreating that which had been terrorized by the kingdom of Sin and Death. Recreation doesn't have to wait until the Lord returns in glory. To be sure, it's only on that day that *everything* will finally be put right, but we can begin now to experience the joy that comes from being recreated. St. Paul writes, "Therefore, if any one is in Christ, he *is* a new creation; the old has passed away, behold, the new has come" (2 Corinthians 5:17, emphasis mine).

Many people live with the lie that says, "This is just the way I am. I'm stuck, defined by my past, caught in my addictions." Or we say these things about others, perhaps even those we love. "Well, that's Bob. He's always been that way, and he always will be."

No! The whole principle of the Christian life is that *you can change*. Not by "trying harder" but because the Holy Spirit, who is given to us, enables us to become new creations. The power that raised Jesus from the dead dwells in you! And by that power at work in our lives, we can say, "I *used* to live that way, but I don't live that way anymore. Not because I 'tried' but because I surrendered. I invited the Lord into my life, and now I live in freedom."

There's an amazing nebula in the universe called the Orion Nebula, and it's essentially a star-making factory. Scientists actually refer to it as a "star nursery." (Google it; you've got to see it!) God is still creating stars today, but even more wondrously, He is recreating you and me. Your marriage, your personal life, your friendships, your pain . . . it can all be recreated. Even if you feel locked in bitterness, resentment, a desire for vengeance, or an addiction to porn, gambling, drinking, or something else, God can recreate you, forgive you, make you forgiving, and set you free. He has that power, and you have that opportunity, thanks to Jesus' death and resurrection.

The Sixth Difference: Jesus Has Rendered Sin Impotent

This one can be harder to understand, but I'll simplify it. Essentially, this means, "We don't have to sin."

Don't get me wrong—we *do* sin all the time because we have memories, bad habits, and the inclination to sin, as a result of the fall. But we don't *have* to sin. The One who made the universe and who raised Jesus from the dead lives in us. That means we don't have to speak the way we used to speak, and we don't have to think or act the way we used to think or act. *We can change.* Sin has no tyranny, no stronghold, no rule over us anymore.

As St. Paul puts it in Romans 6:6-7,

We know that our old self was crucified with him so that the sinful body might be destroyed, and we might no longer be enslaved to sin. For he who has died is freed from sin.

Paul is referring to the dominion of (capital S) Sin here. This dominion has been defeated. Thus, he can go on to say:

So you also must consider yourselves dead to sin and alive to God in Christ Jesus.

Let not sin therefore reign in your mortal bodies, to make you obey their passions. Do not yield your members to sin as instruments of wickedness, but yield yourselves to God as men who have been brought from death to life, and your members to God as instruments of righteousness. For sin will have no dominion over you. (Romans 6:11-14)

You can see how this list of differences is a set of building blocks: we were transferred from the rule of darkness, we were given access to God the Father, we were recreated by the power of the Holy Spirit who raised Jesus from the dead and who dwells with us, and we can now live entirely new lives, no longer stuck in the sinful ways and habits of our pasts.

The Seventh Difference: Jesus Has Given Us Authority over the Enemy

In Luke 10:19, when Jesus sends out the seventy-two, he says to them, "Behold, I have given you authority to tread upon serpents and scorpions, and over all the power of the enemy; and nothing shall hurt you."

Remember, Scripture tells us not only what happened but what *always* happens. This is Jesus speaking to *you*, right now. He gives *you* authority; He gives *you* power. What does that look like? It doesn't mean you should literally trample on snakes and scorpions. Rather, recall those questions I asked in chapter 8 when I encouraged you to ask the Holy Spirit to shine a bright light and expose where the enemy is trying to work in your life at this moment:

- Where is the enemy accusing me right now?
- What lie is crippling me right now?

The authority Jesus gives you means that when Satan accuses and lies to you, you are not defenseless! When the taunts, accusations, and lies come, you can take authority over the enemy and his evil spirits. You can say things like "In the name of Jesus, I renounce the lie that I'm worthless . . . , the lie that I am not loved . . . , the lie that I am disposable . . . , the lie that I'm a bad father or mother . . . , the lie that I'm a bad wife or husband . . . , the lie that I'm a bad priest. In the name of Jesus, I take authority against the spirit of guilt that is accusing me and I bind you and cast you to the foot of the cross for Jesus to do with as he wishes."

You have authority over the enemy as a result of what Jesus has done for you on the cross. You are not helpless in this battle that is life. Use that authority daily! Jesus has given it to you.

The Eighth Difference: Jesus Has Sent Us on Mission to Get His World Back

The Latin Mass ends with the words *Ite, missa est*. The best translation I've heard of this is "She is sent." Who's the "she"?

The Church! And who's the Church? Not simply bishops or the hierarchy, but all of us who have been baptized and incorporated into Christ. Who's doing the sending? God. What's the mission? To get His world back.

Outside my old parish, as people drove away, they saw signs that said, "You are now entering mission territory." Every time we leave Mass, we're commissioned by God to go into the world, share the gospel, and be on the attack. But the attack is not against other people, many of whom have been blinded by the ruler of this world, just as I was once blinded. Other people are *not* the enemy. Satan is.

There's a frequently cited passage in Matthew that is pertinent here, but I don't think we always use it correctly. Matthew 16:18 says,

> And I tell you, you are Peter, and on this rock I will build my church, and the gates of Hades will not prevail against it. (NRSVCE)

We often interpret that to mean, "Well, I guess no matter how bad it gets, the Church will never collapse." But that's not what this passage means. Read it closely. Have you ever been attacked by a gate? Of course not. Gates aren't offensive measures; they're *defensive* measures. We, the Church—you and I—are the ones on the attack. We are storming the gates of Hell (or are supposed to be!), not vice versa.

We Christians too often live with a defeatist attitude. The Power that created the universe, that crushed Death and Sin, Satan and Hell, lives in *you* and wants to use *you*. Hell can't compete with God. So share the gospel with joy, love, and confidence. Lift up what God has done for you in Jesus. Share with others the only news that enables them to break out of a culture riddled with despair, a culture that's literally killing itself because it doesn't think life is worth living. Jesus tells us, the Church, "Hell doesn't have a chance. So get out there. *Go!*"

It's right there in Scripture, telling us what happened and what always happens:

And he said to them, "Go into all the world and preach the gospel to the whole creation." (Mark 16:15)

And what is the gospel?

Created. Captured. Rescued. Response. When you know those four words, you know the gospel.

And hopefully you not only know the story of the gospel, but you have *experienced* or are *ready* to experience it: to meet Him, to *know* Him, to be transferred from slavery to freedom, and to set out on a mission for Him:

And Jesus came and said to them, "All authority in heaven and on earth has been given to me. Go therefore and make disciples of all nations, baptizing them in the name of the Father and of the Son and of the Holy Spirit, teaching them to observe all that I have commanded you; and lo, I am with you always, to the close of the age." (Matthew 28:18-20)

Regardless of how bleak the world (or the Church) looks, here is the truth: Jesus is *Lord*. And to say that Jesus is Lord means that *nobody else is*, no matter how it may appear right now.

Earlier I shared a quote from C. S. Lewis. "Christianity is the story of how the rightful king has landed, you might say landed in disguise."[34] He added, "And is calling us all to take part in a great campaign of *sabotage*."[35] I love this quote! This is what God is calling you and me to do: freed from the power of Death, no longer held under the dominion of the kingdom of darkness and Sin, recreated by the Holy Spirit, and given authority from Jesus, we are now equipped to fight. We are armed with love, truth, goodness, beauty, forgiveness, and all the weapons of the kingdom of God. We're called to undo—to sabotage—what the enemy has wrought ever since that fateful day in Eden so long ago.

In the next section, we'll explore this mission in more detail. It's a crucial part of the response we're called to make as disciples of Jesus and in gratitude for all that He has done for us.

CHAPTER 14

The Heart
of the Gospel

Before we explore our response to what Jesus has done for us, let me offer a final thought on the concept of being rescued.

I recently gave a retreat on these topics, and during a break, a man approached me, obviously befuddled, and said, "Father, I've heard everything you said, and I think I understand it. There's only one thing I *don't* understand. Why? Why would God do this? How can it be that the Creator of the universe, which is an unfathomable ninety-plus billion light years across, would become man and do all of this for us?"

I told him what I'll tell you. It's simply this: because you and I matter to God. Why that is, I honestly don't know. God doesn't need me or you. He's not bored. He's infinitely happy. And yet He not only *loves* us, but He *thirsts* for us.

Mother Teresa used to have two words painted beside the crucifixes in all the chapels of the Missionaries of Charity around the world: "I thirst." These were words Jesus spoke from the cross. Mother often reminded the sisters that to say

"I thirst" does not simply mean "I love you." It means "I *want* you. I *desire* you." Somehow, in a way we cannot fathom, *God* thirsts for and desires *us*. You. Me. How else can we explain the cross of Jesus?

I also shared with that man something I came across many years ago but can no longer recall where. Someone was trying to explain to a friend what it means to say "I love you." "It means," the person said, "you are worth the trouble." When a mother gets up at night to feed and care for her crying child, she does it because that child is worth the trouble. When a doctor rushes to the hospital in the middle of the night to treat a patient who was just injured, he does it because that person is worth the trouble. And Jesus from the cross says to you and to me, "*You* are worth the trouble. You are worth My becoming man, being scourged, crowned with thorns, and going to the cross. You are worth dying for. You *matter* to Me!"

Maybe we can simply answer that man's question this way: "Because love does such things. And God *is* love."

There is a beautiful icon—a favorite image in the Eastern Church—that is called the *Anastasis*, the Greek word for "resurrection." It's worth looking up, so that you can see its beauty. Jesus is at the center—risen, glorious, triumphant. No longer is His divinity hidden; it is shining forth. This is Jesus as He really is, blinding and brilliant. And He is standing on Satan's head. At His feet are locks and keys, the ones that held our race bound. And on one side of him is a man, whose hand Jesus is holding. On the other side, Jesus is holding the hand of a woman. They are Adam and Eve, and Jesus is leading them out of Hell.

Right now, Jesus stretches out His hand to you too. He invites you to grab it, hold on, and let Him lead. Whatever prison, tomb, or hell you're in, take His hand. He can deliver you from wherever you are, give you grace to suffer well if that's what you need, and deliver you from bitterness and resentment. He can bring warmth into a heart that's grown cold. Whatever it is, He can do it. All you have to do is take His hand. He is utterly unconquerable. You can have unshakable confidence in Him.

Do You Know What I Have Done for You?

In chapter 8, we read about the image of the trafficker and the helpless victim. You asked the Holy Spirit to help you imagine being in that dire, hopeless situation when suddenly someone enters the room and unties you. As you near the exit, aware of the fact that the tyrant is on the other side, you are filled with exhilaration but also fear. And as you cross the threshold, your rescuer points to the tyrant, now completely and utterly bound. And your rescuer, Jesus, says, "You don't have to worry about him anymore. I took care of him." And out you go. Into the light. Into freedom. Into a new life.

What do you give a man like that? What's the appropriate or logical response when someone rescues you from Hell and saves you from unending Death?

Let's find out.

Summary of Part III: Rescued

- God's response to our captivity to Sin is shocking and unexpected.
- In short, He rescued us and released us from our chains.
- Why did Jesus come? He "landed" on the earth to fight our enemy, the devil.
- What was Jesus doing on the cross? Jesus is the hunter, not the hunted; the aggressor, not the victim. He is the ultimate Ambush Predator. The crucifixion could not have happened unless God wanted it to.
- What difference does it all make? Jesus has humiliated the enemy, destroyed Death, transferred us to His kingdom, given us access to the Father, recreated us, rendered Sin impotent, and given us authority over the enemy.
- He now sends us on a mission to get his world back.

Discussion Questions:

1. Does knowing that Jesus is not a victim but a hunter—that He is actually *the* Ambush Predator—change the way you see the Passion?
2. Are you afraid to die? Do you feel differently about death now?
3. When you hear about "the love of God," do you hear a cliché? Or do those words have a deeper meaning for you? Do you genuinely believe you're "worth the trouble"?

If you are so inclined, you might want to try praying this prayer:

Father,

I believe that out of Your infinite love You created me. I come before You, just as I am, with all my brokenness, wounds, and hurts. I am sorry for all the times I have believed the enemy's lies that You are not a good Father and don't love me. I repent and ask You to forgive me for all of my sins.

Jesus,

Thank you for coming to rescue me from Sin, Death, Hell, and Satan. I surrender to You right now and invite You to be Lord over every area of my entire life.

Come, Holy Spirit,

Flood my soul with the love of the Father and convince me that I matter, I'm worth the trouble, and that in God's eyes I'm worth dying for.

Come, Holy Spirit...

PART IV

Response

Ask for the graces of gratitude, surrender, and courage.

CHAPTER 15

Our Personal Response to Jesus: Gratitude, Surrender, and Courage

"Every day I think about what you
said to me that day on the bridge."
—*Saving Private Ryan*

One of the most moving cinematic moments of all time is the ending of *Saving Private Ryan*. In the film's closing minutes, a now-elderly James Ryan crouches before the grave of Captain John Miller. Ryan has returned to Normandy where he and others landed on June 6, 1944 to free a continent oppressed and tyrannized by a demonical dictator. From the monologue that follows, we learn that this is the first time Ryan has visited the grave of the man who saved his life.

The movie opens with the elderly Ryan heading to that cemetery, but most of the film is a flashback that tells the story of young Private Ryan, who has just lost his three brothers who were also serving in the war. Upon learning about the deaths of so many in one family, the Army chief of staff sends a team of soldiers, led by Captain Miller, to find Ryan, rescue him, and send him back home so that his mother might not lose all of her sons to war. The movie reaches a climax in a small town in France, where the Germans have the squad cornered. Captain Miller dies after a heroic act, but just before he dies, Private Ryan goes to his side. The men look at one another, and Miller mouths something that Ryan can't hear.

"What, sir?" Ryan asks.

Miller, struggling to speak and breathe, pulls Ryan close and whispers in his ear, "James, earn this."

Ryan pulls back, and the two men look directly into each other's eyes. "Earn it," Miller says. And with that, he breathes his last.

The final scene of the movie returns us to the cemetery in Normandy. James Ryan has come on a mission of sorts. His wife, children, and grandchildren accompany him, but they stand a respectful distance away as Ryan approaches the grave of Captain Miller. He crouches in front of the white cross that marks Miller's grave, and he says,

My family is with me today. They wanted to come with me. To be honest with you, I wasn't sure about how I'd feel coming back here. Every day I think about what you said to me that day on the bridge. I've tried to live my life the best I could. I hope that was enough. I hope that at least in your eyes, I've earned what all of you have done for me.

His wife seems unaware of who Miller was and what he did, let alone the fact that she would not have married Ryan if the man buried there hadn't done what he did to rescue him. Though Ryan, like so many war veterans, never shared the story of how he was saved, from his heartfelt words, we know that he had thought every day about what Miller said to him. He had tried to make his entire life a response to the heroism and sacrificial love Miller had displayed.

"Love?" you may ask. Yes, love. For "Greater love has no man than this," Jesus tells us, "that a man lay down his life for his friends" (John 15:13).

That scene is one of the most powerful depictions I know to help us understand how we should live our lives in response to what Jesus—the greatest of "war veterans"—has done for us. Of course, there is a critical difference. Jesus didn't say from the cross, "Earn this." No one could possibly "earn" God's love, the Incarnation, or our rescue from Sin, Death, Satan, and Hell. But Private Ryan's response should provoke a question in us all: "Do we think *every day* about what Jesus has done for us?" Or has His rescue been taken for granted? How many times have we entered a church and failed to stop in our tracks at the sight of the crucifix or passed a crucifix in our own homes without giving it a thought?

As we explore our response to Jesus, the graces to request from the Holy Spirit are these: *gratitude* for all that God has done for us in Jesus, *surrender* to Jesus as Lord, and the *courage* to help God get his world back.

Agents of Sabotage

Before we dig deeper into our response to Jesus' extraordinary gift of self, I want to make something clear. We often hear that our goal as Christians is to "get to heaven." Of course we should desire to reach heaven, but there's more to our Christian lives than that. The rescue mission of Jesus is twofold: it is for us personally, *and* it's something that's supposed to *continue through us*. In other words, Jesus' rescue is something that *I receive* and something I'm *called to spread* in my daily life. Our response, then, includes worship, thanksgiving, and surrender, as a personal response, and it also includes being a *herald* of what God has done for us in Jesus, as a mission response.

In the words of C. S. Lewis, our response to Jesus should make us active agents of sabotage. Our weapons are love, truth, beauty, goodness, and justice. We wield them to continue God's work of recreation and to spread His rescue mission in every sphere of influence in our lives. While creation will only be fully restored when the rightful King returns and puts everything right, that doesn't mean that there isn't work for you and me to do right now. We should strive to bring everything we touch and encounter back into conformity with the Father's original intent.

So in this section, we'll look at

- our personal response to Jesus (worship, praise and thanksgiving, surrender),

- how He's sending us out on a mission and how to do that more effectively,
- a suggestion for my brother priests (and for bishops and deacons), and
- a hope-filled and encouraging reflection from a friend to inspire us as we are sent out into the world.

In many ways, this section is the most important because God has "already done His part," if you will, and it's "our turn." Of course, God doesn't actually barter with us, and we are not called to "earn" anything, but God's great love does call us to a response. He has not only created everything out of nothing and out of His love, but He has rescued His beloved creation and especially His most beloved creature—the human person—in a shocking and unexpected way. He has rescued us personally from a terrible fate so that we can go free and one day share in His abundant, eternal life, where there will be no pain, no tears, and no death.

What good would life have been to us had Christ not come as our Redeemer?

This question is posed in the *Exultet*, the great hymn sung at the beginning of every Easter Vigil. In the darkness of a church lit only by the Paschal candle (which symbolizes Jesus, the light of the world that darkness cannot overcome), the *Exultet* annually asks us to consider the question anew: *What good would life have been to us had Christ not come as our Redeemer?*

Indeed! We were bound by the powers of Sin and Death, destined for eternal futility, but "because love does such things" and because we *matter* to God, as incomprehensible as that may be to us, we've been offered new life and new hope.

The only question that remains is: "How will I respond?"

And our response matters. It is not automatic. At this very moment, God is longing to hear some of you say, "Thank You, Lord! I surrender. I give You my life. Use me to help build Your kingdom and be an agent of sabotage." Even those of us who have lived as disciples of Jesus for years must choose how to respond every single day. A priest I know was asked, "When did you decide to become a priest?" This man, who was ordained twenty-five years ago, replied, "This morning." Every day and throughout each day, we decide how to live our lives. Will we live then no longer for ourselves but for Him, as St. Paul puts it (see 2 Corinthians 5:15)?

Remember the simple but crucial fact that the Christian life is a *response* to what God has already done. God is love, and He has taken the first step; He always does. Now He looks at us with love and asks, "What will you do?"

Will we respond with: "Every day I think about what You did for me"?

First Personal Response: Worship

"You gotta serve somebody," Bob Dylan said. Everyone worships something or someone. I often argue that if you want to see worship in action, you'll find it on an autumn Saturday in college towns across America. In packed stadiums, men, women, and children perform a kind of worship. Jumping up and down, painted faces and bodies, voices hoarse from screaming with happiness over a great play or anger over a call by the referee, bands playing, folks singing, cheerleaders encouraging frenzied yells. There's a communal commitment to winning.

The next day, however, in too many towns, churches can't boast the same kind of attendance or enthusiasm. Saturday's frenzied support devolves into Sunday's subdued or reluctant participation. I am as big a football fan as anyone, and I love a good game. But deep down, we know that a football game means nothing in the grand scheme of things. So why is our response to the God who saved us from our worst nightmares so muted?

I remember one Sunday morning, when the sports networks were rehashing and celebrating a spectacular play that had come at the end of a football game. As a fan, I agreed it was amazing. But as I watched the highlights and listened to the announcers gush over the winning player, I sensed Jesus asking, "Where is My glory?" His tone was both hurt and righteously angry. "They give endless accolades to a young man who won a game," I sensed Him say, "but why does nobody talk about Me that way?" Then, unbelievably, it was as if He showed me a highlight that could never happen.

In my mind I saw a football game. There was one second left on the clock, the losing team on their own one-yard line, down by five points. The quarterback took the snap and fell back into the end zone. No one was open downfield, and suddenly one player after another piled on top of him. Game over! Or it should have been. But as this mental image continued to unfold in my mind, I saw this quarterback struggle forward, despite the defensemen all over him. He refused to go down.

Not only that, but he moved forward. As he made progress, the entire defense was on top of him, a sight that was truly laughable. It isn't possible for a man to stand upright with eleven other men on top of him, but the quarterback kept moving until, finally, he crossed the goal line. There it was: the single greatest play of all time, never to be equaled or outdone. It would be the number one highlight of all time on SportsCenter.

As I watched this play out in my imagination that morning, I felt the Lord say, "That's nothing. I took the sins of the whole world upon My back. I took on Satan and the powers and principalities that held your race bound. And I won!" He said again, "Now, where is My glory?"

Worship is defined as showing honor, reverence, or devotion. Our culture's misplaced worship is a matter of justice. Justice is giving someone what is due them, what they deserve. The simple truth is that no one and nothing deserves the honor, reverence, and devotion that God deserves. Unfortunately, our culture is full of idolatry, with many worshipping the idols of sports, money, status, prestige, pleasure, or sex. I used to think of the ancients, who made and bowed down before statues, as foolish, but then I came across this definition of idolatry from Tim Keller:

What is an idol? It is anything more important to you than God, anything that absorbs your heart and imagination more than God, anything you seek to give you what only God can give. . . . If anything becomes more fundamental than God to your happiness, meaning in life, and identity, then it is an idol.[36]

I thought about all the ways that I seek happiness outside of God and my relationship with Him. Suddenly, I realized I was just like those foolish ancients.

The first thing we're called to do in response to all that God has done for us in Jesus is to worship Him, that is, to give Him the honor, reverence, and devotion He is due, knowing that He is fundamental to our happiness and deserves to fully absorb our lives.

Second Personal Response: Praise and Thanksgiving

Related to worship but distinct from it are praise and thanksgiving. We worship God for who He *is*: for His greatness and splendor, His majesty, beauty, and goodness beyond all telling. We praise and thank God for what He has *done*.

How much of your prayer time is spent praising and thanking God? I can easily fall into the habit of defining prayer as bringing various needs and petitions to God. As if He needed me to tell Him what I want or need! As one commentator put it, the goal of prayer cannot possibly be the communication of information.[37] God knows what we need before we ask!

When you next enter into prayer, try to start by thanking and praising God. If you don't know where to begin, try starting with the psalms. Just as a mother or father has to teach a child how to talk, so God has to teach us how to pray, and the psalms are one of His greatest teaching tools. Some of my favorites for praising and thanking him are Psalms 34, 100, 103, 136, 145, and 150.

Another helpful passage is Exodus 15:1-21, which describes the scene after the Israelites saw the Egyptian army drown in the waters of the Red Sea.[38] As you pray with this passage, I encourage you to perceive it, not as the story of strangers rescued from a foreign dictator, but as *our* story and *our* rescue. The Bible is full of our shared family history. (More on that to come!)

So open your Bible, and open your heart. Let Scripture lead you to praise and thanksgiving. Let the Lord hear your response as you cry out to Him with gratitude for all He has done for you.

Third Personal Response: Surrender

The final way we can personally respond to the extraordinary rescue mission of Jesus is surrender.

We bristle at the concept of surrender because it implies a sort of "giving up." Most of us don't like the idea of relinquishing control. But remember Pope St. John Paul II and his statement that the kerygma is "the initial ardent proclamation by which a person is one day overwhelmed and brought to the decision to entrust himself to Jesus Christ by faith."[39] Surrender is simply another word for "entrust," and both words are another way to say "faith."

But perhaps even more simply, we could ask this question: "What does God want from me?"

The Gospel of John addresses that question. Jesus on the cross utters two words: "I thirst" (John 19:28). For what does Jesus thirst? What is God longing for? He thirsts and longs for us to entrust ourselves to Him, to surrender to Him—*to have faith in Him.*

In the Gospel of Luke, Jesus asks, "When the Son of man comes, will he find faith on earth?" (18:8). In other words, when Jesus returns in glory to the earth, will He find that we responded as we should have to His extraordinary rescue mission? Or will He find that we took His sacrifice and rescue for granted?

If another word for surrender is "faith," let's take a look at what faith actually is. But first, let's define what faith is *not*. Faith is not irrational, blind, contradictory to reason or science, or a mere intellectual assent. Let's take those one at a time.

As I mentioned in chapter 2, many people in our modern Western culture seem to think that having faith means checking one's intelligence at the door. They separate people into two categories. On one side they place those who are intelligent, logical, reasonable, and well-educated. On the other side? People of faith. The implication is that believers are unintelligent, illogical, irrational, and uneducated. This is untrue. Remember, the Church has always believed that we must employ our intellect and reason and has always been at the forefront of higher education. God gave us reason for a reason!

Second, some say that faith is blind. I once heard a sports announcer talking about a football team that was really struggling. The coach had said he believed the team would turn a corner soon and have a great season, even though realistically that was impossible. The announcer concluded, "I guess that's what faith is. Faith is belief in the absence of evidence."

Absolutely not! That coach's "belief" in the absence of evidence was nothing more than fantasy. It was blind, illogical, and irrational—and that's not faith. As the Church teaches, faith is not blind but is actually a *way* of knowing and a *way* of seeing. In fact, to *not* have faith is to be blind. To not have the power of the Holy Spirit alive within us is to be unable to see reality as it is.

Third, faith is not contradictory to reason or science. As Pope St. John Paul II wrote in *Fides et Ratio*, faith and reason are two ways of seeking the same thing: truth (1). Truth is not a thing or a theorem. Truth is a person. As Jesus says, "I am the way, and the truth, and the life" (John 14:6). So faith and reason (or faith and science) are complementary ways of understanding reality and arriving at knowledge. Faith *without* reason is simply superstition or, as I mentioned above, fantasy. That's dangerous, to be sure, but not as dangerous as reason without faith, which, as Pope St. John Paul II pointed out in *Fides et Ratio*, leads to nihilism and to relativism (46).

A final point on what faith is not: faith is not the mere intellectual assent that there is a God. As the Letter of James reminds us, "Even the demons believe" (2:19). To simply acknowledge, "Yeah, I think God is real" isn't faith. Relationships require more than mere intellectual assent to the existence of the other person.

So what *is* faith? In the words of a priest friend and mentor who is now passed away, faith is this: leaning so far over on God that if He weren't there, you'd fall down. In other words, faith is a personal, wholehearted connection to God—a connection that involves my whole life. I don't merely give parts of my life to God; I strive to bring my whole life into this personal surrender to Jesus. Another way my friend described faith was as God's work in me to which I respond. I've always loved that definition.

Faith is first of all a gift. That gift is God's work in me; it is the Holy Spirit, who enables me to see more than just the historical data about Jesus. That gift brings me to the point of understanding that Jesus is God and that He laid down His life for me. And the follow-up to my friend's definition is that my new understanding—that personal, wholehearted connection—is something I *have* to respond to. How could I not?

And that's what we're now zeroing in on. Ask yourself, "What's the reasonable, logical, and intelligent response to a God who is so grand that He made a universe that's ninety-plus billion light years across?" A God deemed great not only because of the magnitude of His creation but because of His *love*? He is a God who loves so deeply that He humbled Himself to become flesh, disguised Himself to go into battle, bound the strong one, crushed the powers of Sin and Death, and laid down His life for us and rose from the dead who is now preparing a place for you and me and will come back to create a new heaven and a new earth. What's the reasonable response to a God who does all that?

Isn't it to give Him *everything*?

Here's how the *Catechism of the Catholic Church* describes faith:

> By faith man completely submits his intellect and his will to God. With his whole being man gives his assent to God the revealer. Sacred Scripture calls this human response to God, the author of revelation, "the obedience of faith." (143, cf. Romans 1:5; 16:26)

This response is an ongoing battle, of course, for all of us. I daily have to submit my will to God. My experience personally and in pastorally caring for many people is that there are two conversions in most of us. There's a conversion of the intellect and a conversion of the will. Oftentimes these are many years apart. It's easy for my mind to surrender to God: to grasp the truth about Him. It's far more difficult to surrender my *will* to God. It's a daily struggle. In the Letter to the Romans, St. Paul encourages us to offer our bodies "as a living sacrifice" to God (12:1). It's commonly observed that the problem with a living sacrifice is that it keeps crawling off the altar.

Every day I must deliberately crawl back on the altar and say, "Lord, here I am. I trust You; help me to trust You more. I love You; help me to love You more. I surrender to You; help me to surrender to You more. Because I know no one loves me as You do, and no one's deserving of my trust the way You are. Help me to give You everything *again*."

As the *Catechism* says, "Faith is first of all a personal adherence of man to God" (150). *Personal*. It's not merely intellectual and not merely a "part" of me. It's *all* of me. And the model of faith is Mary. I've often been struck by the incredible insight of artists who have painted the Annunciation (that moment when God invited Mary to say yes to His invitation to be the mother of His only begotten Son). Most have depicted Mary as reading Scripture. Have you ever wondered what enabled Mary to respond as she did, saying to the archangel Gabriel, "Behold, I am the handmaid of the Lord; let it be to me according to your word" (Luke 1:38)? More colloquially, she said, "I'm entirely Yours, God. Do with me whatever You want." Certainly, she was conceived without Sin, so it's easy to dismissively say, "Well, it must have been easy for her." But Eve was also conceived without Sin, and it wasn't so easy for her! The Church has always seen Mary as the new Eve, so let's compare them.

Who was Eve? Eve was immaculately conceived, created without Sin. She was betrothed to a man and visited by an angel. After the visit from that fallen angel, Eve was disobedient to God, and the result of her disobedience was death for the human race.

Who is Mary? Mary was also conceived without Sin, betrothed to a man, and visited by an angel who delivered a message. In contrast to Eve, Mary was obedient to the message, and the result is *life* for the human race. So what enabled Mary to say yes? There's no definitive answer, but here's what I think. Those artists had it right. Mary was able to surrender to God because she knew God's word. She saw His faithfulness to the covenant He'd made all the way back to Adam and Eve. Even on the day of our first parents' rebellion, God promised that He would put enmity between the woman and her offspring and the serpent and his offspring. He promised that Sin and Death and the serpent would not have the last word. That was the promise of the gospel, and Mary was familiar with all the stories (what we now know as the Old Testament) of God's promises to and interactions with His people. And because she had seen His faithfulness, love, and mercy, when Gabriel came, she was able to surrender.

So let's ask Mary to help us know her Son, Jesus, more clearly and to help us know the faithfulness of God the Father more clearly. Ask Mary to pray for you, to help you see and understand that He is a good Father who loves us beyond all telling and that her Son is a merciful, faithful high priest who calls us brothers and sisters, who even now is interceding for us before that good Father's throne.

CHAPTER 16

The Mission Response

Now that we know we are recipients of the gospel and respond personally through worship, praise and thanksgiving, and surrender, let's turn to the other facet of our response: our call to be an agent in sharing the gospel. This is the Great Commission given at the end of the Gospel of Matthew:

> And Jesus came and said to them, "All authority in heaven and on earth has been given to me. Go therefore and make disciples of all nations, baptizing them in the name of the Father and of the Son and of the Holy Spirit, teaching them to observe all that I have commanded you; and lo, I am with you always, to the close of the age." (28:18-20)

With this, Jesus commissioned all of us—not just his apostles but *all of us*—to be heralds of the gospel. God did not become a man, lay down His life, bind the strong man, and crush the powers of Sin and Death so that only a handful of people would know about it. God desires everyone to know about His rescue because He desires that everyone be saved. But how can others believe in and surrender to Him if they don't hear about Him? They will hear only if heralds are sent forth. God is sending us into a world that is panicked, fearful, and anxious because it does not know Him. The world doesn't even know that there *is* a God, much less that He's a good Father who's done something about the mess we're in. It's the job of the herald to let people know there are reasons to have unshakable confidence in Jesus.

Remember the simple way to share the gospel? Four words:

Created

Captured

Rescued

Response

Heralds take these four words and use them to tell God's story in a way that is unique to them and their life circumstances, while keeping these four basic components in mind. As heralds, we share the news of the "initial ardent proclamation" of the gospel that leads to surrendering to Jesus in faith, and as we do—as happens so often when I share it—it moves someone to tears and provokes the response, "That's not the God I knew growing up. Tell me more."

As we do that, we're being faithful to the "mission" portion of our response. We're called to be active agents in the liberation, or rescue mission, that Jesus carried out for us. In other words, Jesus' resurrection and his outpouring of the Holy Spirit upon us not only began the process of transformation in *our* lives, but it is also the means by which the process of transformation can continue in the lives of *others*.

One way to think of this is to recall that trafficker we talked about in chapter 8. Imagine again that you are the victim who has just been rescued. If you were the only prisoner, you'd walk away with your savior, grateful for your freedom, not looking back. But what if there were other women there? You'd want them rescued too. Your first response—thanking and praising your rescuer for what he's done for you—would then give way to the next step: how to rescue those other women. What can you do, along with the one who saved you, to get everyone out?

Another helpful way to understand our call to mission is through a passage in the first chapter of the Acts of the Apostles. There's a scene I actually find rather comical. As the apostles watch Jesus ascend into heaven, two men who are actually angels appear by their sides. In Acts 1:11, the angels say, "Men of Galilee, why do you stand looking into heaven?" I imagine those angels looking at the apostles—who are gawking at the heavens even after Jesus has disappeared from their sight—shaking their heads, dumbfounded at how inert the apostles are and tapping the apostles on the shoulder. "Hey, guys," I imagine them saying, "why are you wasting time staring at the sky? C'mon! You've got things to do. Get out there and *get to work*."

As the biblical scholar N. T. Wright frequently reminds us, the message of Easter is not that Jesus has risen and therefore we will too, one day. That is *not* the Easter proclamation of the gospels! It is so much more. The Easter proclamation is "Jesus has risen. There's *work* for you and me to do."

How should we understand that? The most salient point is that Easter is the *beginning* of the recreation of all things. Of course this will only fully happen when Jesus returns in glory. As He says in Revelation, "Behold, I make all things new" (21:5). That's what He began on Easter Sunday, and He will do it fully one day when the rightful King returns to this earth. But even now, you and I are called to work and build for the kingdom in every sphere of our lives: our marriages, our families and friendships, education, the judicial system, health care, institutions—every structure we touch or are part of, all for the glory of God. That might seem like a pipe dream, beyond what we could reasonably expect any individual or even the Church to be able to do, but it's not a mere dream!

The proof that we can run an amazing race from a seemingly impossible and humble starting position is evident in the early Church, so let's take a look at the history of the Church, which is really our collective family history.

Our Family Scrapbook: Knowing Our History, Knowing the Story

Are you intrigued by genealogy? I am. My oldest sister is an amateur genealogist, and she's been gathering data on our family that, in some cases, goes back to the sixteenth century. It's been fascinating for me to learn about bits and pieces of my family tree. While some branches were encouraging and hopeful, others were downright scandalous, but they were always intriguing.

As Christians, we need to know our family history too. Pentecost—when the Holy Spirit descended upon the apostles and Mary and then sent them out to share the gospel with others—is considered the "birthday" of the Church. Something completely new happened. These people who had previously been timid, fearful, and even cowardly—who had abandoned Jesus in what seemed like "the end"—were now literally empowered with a divine spirit. They were radically transformed, enabled to go out into the world to proclaim to others what God had done for them and what He wants to do for others. Why? Because God wants to use us—His family—as the means by which the work of Jesus, the liberation He accomplished for us, will be carried to the ends of the earth.

God could have chosen to do this without any help from you and me, but for some reason, He didn't. He *wants* to use us. Pondering how God used the birthday of the Church to commission the first apostles—a small band of followers—offers tremendous hope and encouragement about how He commissions us today.

In the early nineties, I was fortunate to study in Rome for four years. I routinely walked to the Colosseum, and one of my favorite areas was a wall of maps that showed the growth and expansion of the Roman Empire from the eighth century BC to its height in 117 AD. It was awe inspiring to see the vast, enormous power and influence of Rome, which was an unlikely city to have become the center of the world. There had been nothing spectacular or extraordinary about Rome—not its natural resources nor the weather; in fact, malaria was rampant for hundreds of years. How did this tiny village of huts become the center of the world? It grew for a variety of reasons, but primarily because of the Roman legion, the most powerful army in the world. In other words, it grew through force and violence. A lust for land, resources, wealth, and slaves fueled the legion as it fanned out and conquered foreign lands.

And now let's picture another map: the spread of Christianity from its birthday on Pentecost to the end of the fourth century. Like Rome, Jerusalem was an unlikely candidate to become the center of a worldwide movement. I am fortunate to have gone to the Holy Land several times, but if you didn't know it was the Holy Land, you might simply see it as a dumpy, insignificant little hill town stuck in the desert. And yet, from that unlikely spot, the Church grew and spread like wildfire. And here's what's both unbelievable and significant about that: from the year 64 AD, when Nero's persecution of Christians began, until the year 312 AD, it was officially forbidden to be a Christian in the Roman Empire. Christianity, scorned as a superstition, was illegal. During these 250 years of growth, there were even some periods during which the emperor issued a command that bishops, priests, and deacons be killed on sight. And yet Christianity grew and spread as a powerful force to be reckoned with.

How and why did the Church, our family, grow? Unlike the Roman Empire, it wasn't by force and violence. Christianity grew because Christians fanned out from Jerusalem to spread the word about Jesus, who had stunned them by being crucified and rising from the dead. And here's a simple but often unrecognized observation: before this time, there was no such thing as mission work. Pagans didn't travel to foreign lands to spread the word about Zeus or Apollo. They may have talked about their gods, but they didn't leave home with the intention of sharing their beliefs. Christians did. Why? Revisionist historians might say evangelization is always an attempt to colonize nations, and tragically, that might have happened much later in history. But the first missionaries weren't doing that. They were a small, persecuted band, so why leave home? Why go to foreign lands where they had to learn new languages? What was their agenda? Simply this: freedom, liberation, mercy, and love.

They were eager to tell everyone they met that the world's shipwreck was at an end because someone had done something about Death and Sin. They had experienced this themselves and wanted everyone they met to experience it as well. But Christianity didn't grow only through the early Christians' words. It grew primarily because of the witness of their lives and the impact the gospel made on the entire culture—an impact that made everything more human.

Christian life was clearly radically different from life in the Roman Empire. In a world filled with despair, Christian life was hopeful and joyful, marked by an intense, revolutionary love that was evident in action. That evidence in *action*, not just words, was vital for the growth of the early Church. I propose that in our day and age, it is vital once again.

When I was a pastor and fortunate to have a parish school, I often spent time in the classrooms. One day, the students were having debates, and one of them was about Jesus. I talked with one of the students later, and he had a ton of questions, most of which boiled down to this: "What are the reasons to believe that Jesus is the Son of God?" That's an excellent question. As Christians, we certainly must offer answers to that question. One answer is that the only historically plausible explanation for the growth of Christianity is that Jesus of Nazareth, who was known to be crucified, died, and buried, was later seen bodily—upright, resurrected, and walking around—by a number of people on multiple occasions. He was seen by many who were not his disciples, including a man named Saul. There are many great resources out there to help us understand why the resurrection is historically credible, and if you want to look at Christianity through the lens of reason, that's certainly a starting point.

But here's the challenge: one doesn't become a Christian by the use of reason alone. As important as the intellect is, we don't "think our way" into faith because Christianity isn't primarily a matter of intellectual debate. The early Church grew, and the Church continues to grow when people are impacted by the witness of genuinely Christian lives: lives that are radically different, lives that lead to profound changes in the culture, and lives that, as reported in the Acts of the Apostles, turned the world upside down. *That's* what people said about the early Church: "These people are turning the world upside down!"

The early Church—our family—grew by radically transforming the culture around it. The early Christians imbued daily life with the power of the gospel, making everything about it new and more human. Sadly, many people today hear the word "Christian" and think "repressive" or "restrictive." But if Christianity were nothing more than a repressive regime, how would it have grown as it did without violence and coercion? We desperately need to relearn our family history, which is the history of hearts that have been radically transformed.

Signs of Faith

I once read a story about an atheist who came to faith through the witness of Christians who were living radically altered lives. This man went to work amongst the poorest of the poor in violent, crime-ridden areas. He evangelized in the slums, working with drug lords, prostitutes, pimps, and rival gang members. Incredible conversions began to take place: healing, reconciliation, and other extraordinary happenings. Somehow the cardinal archbishop of the town heard about it, called him in, and asked, "How are you doing what you're doing?" The man said, "Through my own life and my own conversion, I came to be convinced that people need 'signs of faith' that don't require faith."

What are "'signs of faith' that don't require faith"? As this man knew, they are the actions, sacrifices, love, and miracles that are life changing. These are things that nonbelievers witness, and when they do, even if they don't believe in God, at their core they somehow understand that only God could enable such things to happen. This is what happened in the early Church. People saw signs of faith that didn't require faith, and even though they didn't yet believe in the God of Jesus Christ, they knew that only God could be behind such signs.

Let's look at some of those early signs of faith. *First was the care of the sick*. In ancient times, if a plague or epidemic broke out, and especially if you had the financial means, you headed off to your villa in the mountains or down by the sea or wherever you could go to protect yourself. No one thought of rushing in to take care of the sick, especially if they were not relatives and, more especially, if it meant that you yourself could get sick or die. No one, that is, until the Christians. The Christians cared for one another, for those to whom they weren't related, and for those who were not Christians. They did so out of love, mindful of Jesus' command to love one another as He has loved us

A second sign of faith is care for the poor. Three times in the New Testament, St. Paul talks about a collection being taken up for Jewish Christians in Jerusalem by Gentile Christians in other countries. We don't give such things a second thought these days. If you go to church, there's a collection at every Mass, and sometimes there are two or even three. But before the early Christians, no one *ever* took up a collection in one part of the world for unrelated, afflicted foreigners in another part of the world, especially not Gentiles donating their hard-earned money to Jews. It was unheard of, but suddenly—because of the gospel—other human beings were your *family*, so you helped them, even at great personal cost.

Here's another amazing sign of faith: women. According to one sociologist, the single biggest sociological reason for the spread of Christianity in the first few centuries was women. Women flocked to the Church, though that's not exactly the narrative we hear today. The Roman Empire, like most of the ancient world, saw women as fit for one purpose: to produce citizens and soldiers. Women were considered intellectually and physically inferior to men, wives were regularly shared by their Roman husbands, and children were routinely exposed or aborted by the *pater familias* (the male head of household). But the gospel of Jesus Christ brought something revolutionary into the relationship between the sexes. It turned that relationship upside down, just as it was turning the whole world upside down. The gospel transformed the relationship between men and women through the understanding that both are created in the image and likeness of God, both are redeemed by the precious blood of Jesus, and both, while clearly different from one another, are absolutely and radically equal in dignity.

But in the eyes of that former atheist who spoke to his cardinal archbishop, the two biggest "'signs of faith' that don't require faith" are *unity* and *forgiveness*. The early Church grew by demonstrating these two things abundantly and unequivocally.

What do we mean by unity? Jews and Gentiles, formerly hated enemies, began calling each other brother and sister. When Peter entered the house of Cornelius, a Gentile, it was assuredly the first time he had ever stepped into the home of one who was not Jewish (see Acts 10). Imagine how radical that passage of Scripture was for its contemporaries! Jewish teachings of the time said, "Separate yourselves from the Gentiles and do not eat with them and do not perform deeds like theirs and do not become associates of theirs because their deeds are defiled and all their ways are contaminated and despicable and abominable." And yet Peter—compelled by Jesus' command to love, mindful of God's desire to get his world back, and ready to spread the liberating, life-giving message of the gospel—enters the house of a Gentile anyway. Peter brought the good news to Cornelius and his household. He was a herald of the gospel to anyone, Jew or Gentile, who would listen.

Finally, let's look at forgiveness. It's often said that forgiveness is one of the most difficult things to do in life. Forgiveness isn't just difficult; forgiveness is impossible—at least on our own. Left to my own way of thinking, everything inside of me screams for the people who made me suffer when I was a child to pay. If you think Jesus' teaching about loving your enemies is a wonderful little passage, then you've never had an enemy. But if someone has hurt you either mentally or physically, destroyed your reputation, or inflicted any kind of pain or harm on you, then you know that forgiveness does not come naturally. But the early Christians were extraordinary models of forgiveness. Think of St. Paul. One of the factors that must have softened Paul's heart (and also provoked him to no end before he met the risen Jesus on the road to Damascus) was his experience with Stephen. As Stephen was being stoned to death, a sentence for which Saul was at least in part responsible for, Saul heard him pray, "Father, forgive them." Who *does* things like this? And yet the Christian martyrs not only didn't complain when they were being executed, but they *prayed for those who were killing them*. Their witness turned the world upside down.

The early Church understood that Christianity is about more than just inner self-discovery and private devotion, as important as those aspects are. It's also about public witness and rescue. A friend of mine often says, "Rescued people rescue people." When someone experiences the radical transformation that Jesus brings, they can't help but do everything possible to share the message of the gospel one-on-one with others, and to transform institutions, structures, and everything else they encounter in order to help God get His world back.

Of course, to do that is going to provoke hostility because there are still many people who acknowledge lords other than

Jesus. But the early fearless Christians set out, armed with love, to rescue others, and we must do the same. And it's vital that we move forward with *love* because the enemy isn't "the other," however we have defined that, whether it's another political party, race, or gender. The enemy is the enemy. So let's respond to the mission God has given us. Let's be eager to do all we can to share the liberating, life-giving message of the gospel so that all people can experience the freedom that comes from knowing Jesus.

CHAPTER 17

Helping God Get His World Back

Even if we want to share the gospel message, the question usually comes back to this: *How do we actually do this in our daily lives? And what does it look like?*

Recently I was talking with a judge who had heard me speak on this subject. He routinely has to sentence people who've committed serious, violent crimes, and he asked, "How can I be an agent of transformation in my role, from the bench, given the fact that I can't really mention the name of Jesus?" As we discussed it further, he said, "When I am sentencing someone, in their eyes I'm acting in a God-like role, by judging them and 'determining' their future, right? But what if I did something like this? If, for example, I must sentence someone for murder, I could say, 'There are consequences for what you've done. You are going to prison because of the choices you've made, but know this: these choices don't define you; they are not who you are. You're not stuck. You *can* change. You can become a truly great human being.' Would that, in some way, be what you're talking about? Is that how I can try to transform things within my sphere of influence, within my profession? Is that how I can act in a way that helps God get His world back?"

I told him, "Yes, that's *exactly* how we do these things."

Here's another example from my parents' lives. My maternal grandfather abandoned his family, causing terrible pain for my mother, her siblings, and my grandmother. The abandonment was so painful that my mom didn't even speak to my grandfather for many years. She didn't invite him to her wedding, and although he sent gifts, she returned them all unopened. It took many years and a lot of work on my father's part to facilitate healing and reconciliation between my mom and her father, but it finally came. In fact, my mom even ended up caring for my grandfather in his last years.

When my parents married, my dad knew about the tremendous weight of pain Mom carried. He knew that she felt not only the pain of abandonment by her father but also the residual effects of such pain, such as feeling unlovable and rejected, even thinking she was perhaps the cause of the abandonment. My dad knew enough about marriage to understand that God had brought him into Mom's life as a means by which that pain could be healed. And so my father, despite all his shortcomings, lived one of the most heroic lives I've ever seen. He was an extraordinarily successful businessman, but he always said that the priorities in life are simply these: God, family, work. Always in that order. At one point, my dad was in negotiations to save his company, and he had out-of-town meetings every day. It would have been easier for him to stay out of town, but he didn't. Instead, every single night, Dad flew home after exhausting meetings, woke up early in the next morning, prayed, and then got on a plane to do it all over again. He did this for over a month, and he did it for one reason: to be with my mom every night so that her abandonment wounds wouldn't be broken open again.

I could say so many things about the extraordinary love that Dad had for Mom (and vice versa) but I could never put it better than my mother did. Dad passed away a few years before Mom did, and at his funeral, Mom said something I will never forget. Everyone had been seated, except Mom and me. She was in her wheelchair, looking at my dad's casket, and she said, to no one but Dad, "Honey, because of you, I know who God is."

Because of his kindness, patience, gentleness, faithfulness, generosity, compassion, long-suffering, and especially love, he made God tangible and present to my mother. Increasingly, ever since I heard those words a number of years ago, I've thought, "That's the single point of marriage." For those of you who are married, that's one way to start, in terms of transforming a structure so that it comes into harmony with God the Father's original plan. Help God get His world back by simply starting with your marriage. Ask the Lord, "Use me concretely today as an agent of transformation. Bring my marriage ever more into harmony with Your plan." You can do the same thing with your friendships, your parenting, your colleagues, and your job. Make God tangible and present to others, one action and one day at a time.

A Plea

Before I bring this section to a close, I have a plea for my brother priests and deacons (and even bishops if I can be so bold). It's simply this: make time every year at Mass to preach what we're calling here "The Story."

Imagine asking those at Mass on any given Sunday, "How many of you have been overwhelmed by the gospel? And how many of you have made a decision to surrender yourself in faith to Jesus?" How many hands would go up? Not nearly enough. Our flocks, the people whose souls we are responsible for, simply don't hear the entirety of the gospel preached at Mass clearly or often enough.

In many areas of life, we make time to review a variety of things, but we rarely review the gospel in the Church. I suggest that every parish, at least once a year, spend at least four weeks just preaching the gospel in a powerful, compelling way. Beg the Holy Spirit to pour out an anointing upon whoever is preaching so that the hearts of the people can be overwhelmed by the power of the gospel and so that they can make a decision (either anew or for the first time) to surrender themselves to Jesus.

Practically speaking, what does that look like? It could happen at the beginning of the school year or during the Advent season or every January, but whatever time you choose, set aside four consecutive Sundays on which, in addition to proclaiming the lectionary, you simply preach the kerygma. Help people understand why you're doing what you're doing. Let them know you understand that it's hard to go to Mass, hear the Scriptures, and understand how they apply to one's life if they don't first know The Story. Our people need to hear the story of who God is, why He made us, why everything's a mess, what He's done about it, and then—and only then—how they should respond.

The First Evangelization Committee Meeting

It's so easy to feel defeated as a Christian, to see the world and all its misery and think, *What's the use? How can I possibly make an impact? How could we be like the early Church and turn the world upside down?* Everything seems to be too far gone, but that's not actually true. It's worth reminding ourselves that *the gospel is power*, that lives *can* change. Obstacles that seem insurmountable can be removed, and things that seem impossible can happen.

A recently published book captures this line of thought by encouraging us to consider the apostles in the Upper Room at the first evangelization committee meeting shortly after Jesus has ascended.[40] They're all sitting there around a big table, and someone suggests they review the agenda, which is to bring the gospel of Jesus to the world. Their resources:

Bishops: eleven
Priests: same number
Deacons: none
Trained theologians: none
Religious orders: none
Seminarians: none

Seminaries: none
Christian believers: a few hundred
Countries with Christians in them: one
Church buildings: none
Schools and universities: none
Written Gospels: none
Money: very little
Experience in foreign missions: none
Influential contacts in high places: next to none
Societal attitude toward us: ranges from ignorant to hostile

It would have been easy for the apostles to be overwhelmed by discouragement. They faced crises in every direction: vocational, financial, catechetical, educational, and numerical. But they weren't discouraged; they were filled with joy and hope. They had great confidence in their Lord, their message, and the creativity and fertility of the Church. They knew that their task was to let the Holy Spirit use them to grow the Church. They knew the graced means by which it was to grow. And grow it did. As my friend says, the Church today needs the same confidence in the power, goodness, and life-changing potency of the message she bears and in the Church's power of regeneration and growth. Those in positions of influence and authority especially need to be convinced that Christ is the answer to every human ill, the solution to every human problem, and the only hope for a dying race. They need to be convinced of the bad news—that there is nothing we can do by our own power to save ourselves—but they need to be equally convinced of the good news, the *extraordinary* news: that God in His mercy has come among us to set us free from our sins and slavery to the devil. And that for those who turn to their true allegiance, the nightmare of life apart from God can be transformed into the dawn of hope in an eternal destiny. They need to know, from their own experience, that obedience to the gospel is perfect freedom, that holiness leads to happiness, that a world without God is a desolate wasteland, and that new life in Christ transforms darkness into light.

God created the apostles to be alive at the time that Christ came among us. He gave them natural and supernatural gifts and talents so that they would not only encounter Jesus personally, but also respond to Him, go into the world as agents of sabotage and transformation, and do all they could to turn the world upside down. The same God who destined the apostles to be alive at that time has destined you and me to be alive at this time. And just as He gave them gifts, so He's given you and me natural and supernatural gifts. And He's asking us not only to make a personal response to what He's done for us in Jesus, but also to make a more expansive response. He's sending us on a mission. He wants us to tell others about Him and to live as active agents of transforming the world, doing what *we* can to turn it upside down.

It's often noted that we are living the twenty-ninth chapter of the Acts of the Apostles. In other words, the history of the church and the world is still being written right now. It's being written by the Holy Spirit through your life and mine.

And so again with St. Joan, I say to you: Do not be afraid. God is with you. You were born for this.

Summary of Part IV: Response

- What Jesus did for us invites us to gratitude every day.
- Jesus's rescue is something which I *receive* and something I'm *called to spread* as an agent of sabotage.
- Our personal response to Jesus is worship, praise and thanksgiving, and surrender.
- Our personal response is also more expansive: He's sending us out on a mission.
- We start our mission in our own sphere of influence (marriage, friendships, profession).
- We need to know and understand The Story before we can share it.
- Christ is the answer to every human ill, the solution to every human problem.
- God is with us as we try to help Him get His world back.

Discussion Questions

1. Do I consider daily what Jesus has done for me?
2. How do I see my faith? Is it merely private or do I see and understand the idea of a wider mission? Have I ever acted as an "agent of sabotage"?
3. Does the idea of "mission" or "evangelizing" scare me? Why or why not?
4. What does it look like, in my sphere of influence, to help God get His world back?

Notes

1. Fleming Rutledge, *The Crucifixion: Understanding the Death of Jesus Christ* (Grand Rapids, MI: William B. Eerdmans Publishing Company, 2015), 6.
2. https://news.gallup.com/poll/247571/catholics-question-membership-amid-scandal.aspx.
3. Fleming Rutledge, 6.
4. Pope Francis, Apostolic Exhortation *Evangelii Gaudium* [The Joy of the Gospel], November 24, 2013, 165, http://www.vatican.va/content/francesco/en/apost_exhortations/documents/papa-francesco_esortazione-ap_20131124_evangelii-gaudium.html.
5. Pope St. John Paul II, Apostolic Exhortation *Catechesi Tradendae* [Catechesis in Our Time], October 16, 1979, 25.
6. To be clear, if we are to be theologically and biblically accurate, we'd want to add the word "Israel" between "Captured" and "Rescued." It's important to make sure that we see God's faithfulness to the plan He began way back with Abraham, and that Jesus is the fulfillment of all the promises God made throughout the Old Testament. However, as important as this is, I am leaving that for a future work and won't be tackling that all-important point here.
7. Pope St. Paul VI, Dogmatic Constitution on Divine Revelation *Dei Verbum* [Word of God], November 18,1965, 11, https://www.vatican.va/archive/hist_councils/ii_vatican_council/documents/vat-ii_const_19651118_dei-verbum_en.html.
8. *Dei Verbum,* 11.
9. *Dei Verbum,* 12.
10. *Dei Verbum,* 12.
11. *Dei Verbum,* 12.
12. I sometimes fear that people think of reality as something like a Marvel comic: there's a good god, and a bad god, and we humans are down here on earth in the middle of their war, cheering for the good guy to win. That's a comic book world,

not our world. The truth is that the enemy is a creature who was originally created good, just like everything else that exists.

13. "God, who allows himself to be known by human beings through Christ, is the unity of the Trinity: unity in communion. In this way, new light is also thrown on man's image and likeness to God, spoken of in the Book of Genesis. The fact that man, 'created as man and woman,' is the image of God means not only that each of them individually is like God, as a rational and free being. It also means that man and woman, created as a 'unity of the two' in their common humanity, are called to live in a communion of love, and in this way to mirror in the world the communion of love that is in God, through which the Three Persons love each other in the intimate mystery of the one divine life" (St. John Paul II, Apostolic Letter, *Mulieris Dignitatem*, 1988, no. 7).

14. *Catechism*, 391, cf. Lateran Council IV (1215): DS 800.

15. Pope St. John Paul II, Encyclical Letter *Dominum et Vivificantem* [On the Holy Spirit in the Life of the Church and the World], May 18, 1986, 37, 38, http://www.vatican.va/content/john-paul-ii/en/encyclicals/documents/hf_jp-ii_enc_18051986_dominum-et-vivificantem.html.

16. I understand going back and forth between capital and lowercase letters for Sin and Death might be very confusing for some of us. I know it was for me when I first began to understand this! But getting this right is immensely important for understanding both the dire predicament our race was in after the fall, and why the gospel is such extraordinary news. However, we need to do the tough work, especially in St. Paul's letters, of trying to discern when he is talking about sin and death as events that either we commit or happen to us, and when he is talking about them as powers that have been overthrown.

17. Fleming Rutledge, *The Undoing of Death* (Grand Rapids, MI: William B. Eerdmans Publishing Company, 2002), 237.

18. Harold Bloom, ed., *Samuel Beckett's Waiting for Godot: A Tragicomedy in Two Acts* (New York, NY: Bloom's Literary Criticism, 2008), 66.

19. William Stringfellow, *Count It All Joy: Reflections on Faith, Doubt, and Temptation Seen through the Letter of James* (Eugene, OR: Wipf and Stock, 1999), 52.
20. Scott Hahn, *Romans: Catholic Commentary on Sacred Scripture* (Grand Rapids, MI: Baker Publishing Group, 2017), 103.
21. Fleming Rutledge, *The Crucifixion*, 368.
22. English translation of *Benedictus* © 1988 English Language Liturgical Consultation (ELLC). https://www.englishtexts.org/benedictus. Used by permission.
23. C. S. Lewis, *Mere Christianity* (New York, NY: HarperCollins, 2001), 46.
24. F. J. Sheed, *To Know Christ Jesus* (San Francisco, CA: Ignatius Press, 1992).
25. Milton Walsh, *Witness of the Saints: Patristic Readings in the Liturgy of the Hours* (San Francisco, CA: Ignatius Press, 2012), paragraphs 425, 466.
26. *Witness of the Saints*, paragraph 307.
27. *The Sacred Writings of St. Irenaeus* (Altenmunster, Germany: Jazzybee Verlag, 2012), Book V, chapter XVIII, 1.
28. Alistair C. Stewart, trans., *On Pascha: With Fragments of Melito and Other Material Related to the Quartodecimans* (Yonkers, NY: St. Vladimir's Seminary, 2016), Kindle, 100–105.
29. "Victory over the 'prince of this world' (*Jn* 14:23) was won once for all at the Hour when Jesus freely gave Himself up to death to give us His life. This is the judgment of this world, and the prince of this world is 'cast out' (*Jn* 12:31; Rev 1:10)" (*Catechism*, 2853). Although victory over the Devil was won once and for all through the Paschal Mystery, this victory is being worked out in time according to God's Providence. Why God allows the Devil a finite power in the Age of the Church is a "great mystery" (*Catechism*, 395). In a certain sense it is true that the power of the Devil was completely destroyed by Christ's sacrifice on the Cross. This destruction, though, is still being played out in human history.

30. From a letter by St. Braulio, Bishop of Zaragoza, Epistle 19, PL 80,665-666, as appearing in *The Office of the Dead*, https://christbearers.wordpress.com/2012/02/04/the-risen-christ-is-the-hope-of-all-christians/.

31. Scott Hahn, 95.

32. Fleming Rutledge, *The Crucifixion*, 369.

33. To be sure, every human person is created in the image and likeness of God and, as such, is loved by Him. At the same time, Baptism really does something in a person. In fact, it does many things. One of the things it does is to make us a temple of the Holy Spirit, and as Paul reminds us in Romans 8:15 and Galatians 4:6, the Spirit cries out, "Abba! Father!" in us. In other words, one who has been baptized really has a new relationship with God.

34. C. S. Lewis, 46

35. C. S. Lewis, 46

36. Timothy Keller, *Counterfeit Gods: The Empty Promises of Money, Sex, and Power, and the Only Hope that Matters* (New York, NY: Penguin Books, 2009), xxi, xix.

37. Erasmo Leiva-Merikakis, *Fire of Mercy Hearts of the Word: Meditations on the Gospel According to St. Matthew: Vol 1* (San Francisco, CA: Ignatius Press, 1996), 252.

38. Remember that the story of the exodus is the ultimate foreshadowing. It helps us understand what Jesus has done for us. Just as the Israelites were oppressed by Pharaoh, the human race was oppressed by Satan. Just as God dramatically rescued them from slavery through Moses, so too has He rescued us through Jesus. The waters of the Red Sea are an image of the waters of Baptism, making an end of sin and a new beginning of goodness.

39. Pope St. John Paul II, *Catechesi Tradendae*, 25.

40. James Shea, *From Christendom to Apostolic Mission: Pastoral Strategies for an Apostolic Age* (Bismarck, ND: University of Mary, 2020), 36-37.